The Successful Office

The Successful Office

HOW TO CREATE
A WORKSPACE
THAT'S RIGHT FOR YOU

Franklin Becker

ADDISON-WESLEY PUBLISHING COMPANY

Reading, Massachusetts ● Menlo Park, California
London ● Amsterdam ● Don Mills, Ontario ● Sydney

To Zoe and Miles

ISBN 0-201-10153-X
ISBN 0-201-10154-8

ABCDEFGHIJ-DO-85432

First printing, June 1982

ACKNOWLEDGMENTS

All projects have some parts that are more enjoyable than others. For me, one of the real pleasures of writing *The Successful Office* was the opportunity to meet men and women working in all kinds of professions. At first, I did not know what to expect when I walked into a stockbroker's or psychiatrist's or journalist's office. After awhile, one thing became predictable: I would meet friendly and intelligent people, diverse in their views and their work, but generous with their time and ideas. I am indebted to all of them.

Betty Redder, Anne Jones, and Linda Shoemaker typed multiple drafts of the manuscript, keeping their sense of perspective even when I tended to lose mine. Debbie Halpern developed and printed the photographs. Her comments on the photographs and her suggestions for improving them were invaluable. Bill Sims, Beverly Gield, Susan Sayer, and Kenneth Gaylin offered much support and many useful comments. Larry Williams and Bob O'Neal helped clarify and set them in context. Harriet Rubin and Karen Murgolo of Addison-Wesley kept me on track and made many useful editorial changes.

Throughout the whole project my family was marvelous—again. When your children start suggesting book titles ("The Spaghetti Office"), you know they are with you!

Ithaca, New York   F.D.B.
February 1982

The Effect Your Office Has on You

Recently I talked with an executive of a major corporation about how he could redesign his workspace for maximum effectiveness and productivity. To convince him that it was possible, I asked him to tell me about his own office—at home. In contrast to his bland low-key office at work, his home office was paneled in walnut and contained gorgeous leather sofas and chairs and a large executive desk. Diplomas and awards hung on the walls. This was his real personal reserve. It was the place where he felt comfortable, and where much of his best work was done. The irony was that his business office, where he spent twice as much time, was not nearly as effective.

The importance of effective workspaces for our well-being and success is tremendous. From secretary to president, most of us spend more time in our offices than any place else, and how we work depends in large measure on how well our offices work for us. I am an example of that. My office is a bright, pleasant place, very private and personal, orderly, but by no means consistent in design. Its value lies simply in the fact that it fits me. It supports the way I like to work and interact with others.

No one can afford to take for granted the importance of the right office design. If clothing is a second layer of skin, your office environment is a third—you need to dress it (and you) for success. Why should this be so?

A workplace is organized to produce goods and services, but it is also, as the report *Work in America* suggests, the place where we constantly put our self-esteem on the line. The office is where we make every effort to promote and display who we are—or want to be. Work is a pervasive force in shaping our personal identities. It helps bring order and meaning to life, and it helps structure some of our most basic personal relationships.

Creative selection, arrangement, and use of your simple physical surroundings—chairs, tables, storage, lighting, decoration, and other physical elements that comprise your personal office—are a means of enhancing your competence as well as your image. My purpose here is to make you more aware of how your office affects your own behavior and the behavior of others with whom you interact. But first you must think of your office as a fundamental tool of your trade. Why? Because the wrong office will restrict the range of opportunities available to you. Is it worth the headaches, irritation, and tension to let your environment control you?

The ideas and information I offer have evolved from almost fourteen years of research, teaching, and consulting in the area of human-environment relations: the study of how human behavior is influenced by our physical surroundings. Close to one hundred interviews were done especially for this book with architects, stockbrokers, accountants, lawyers, journalists, psychiatrists, professors, and administrators. Their offices influence the way they do their jobs—and with what degree of personal satisfaction. What they do will intrigue and instruct anyone who spends a large portion of their working day in an office—and wished that that office worked better.

The Successful Office draws on examples from small and large business alike. Not all of these are glamorous; but in office terms, beautiful means powerful and functional. All these offices offer tips on how even a rabbit warren can be made more accommodating. Part I, "Taking Office," provides a specially tinted pair of spectacles for looking at the limitations and possibilities of your work environment, and your own work habits. Part 2, "Tools of the Trade," takes on the "Maalox issues," the ones we experience stress over: privacy, power, and status. How do colors, furniture arrangement, equipment, and decorations raise your visibility, or minimize it when you really need to be alone? Part 3, "Styles of Office," leads you inside actual working offices of writers, doctors, artists, therapists, and many others. These individual offices point out the special needs and problems of different styles of offices, from client-centered and administrative to creative. The book's concluding section provides a glimpse into the future, and shows how computers can be used to accommodate diverse workstyles. In the future, one size will not fit all.

Nor does one style fit all right now. Read on, and realize that there is more to your work area than a desk and a chair. Much more.

CONTENTS

PART ONE

Taking Office

CHAPTER ONE

Workstyles

Plumbers have wrenches; surgeons, scalpels; carpenters, hammers and chisels: the tools of their trades. Good tools make for good work. For knowledge workers—lawyers, writers, executives, accountants, professors, managers, therapists, stockbrokers, journalists, people who work with ideas and information rather than with wood, pipe, concrete, or steel—the tools of the trade are the office and all its equipment and furnishings. In fact, your office can be as important to your job as a scalpel is to a surgeon. When you realize this fact, you will take your office more seriously. You will become aware of the whole psychology of workspaces and workstyles that extend far beyond the conventions of decoration or design.

P-PLACES AND O-PLACES

Offices tend to be either people places (P-places) or object places (O-places). P-places acknowledge human diversity, encourage individual differences, and are vividly personal. O-places treat individuals as interchangeable parts, conceal individual differences, and are standardized and impersonal. P-places make good tools for knowledge workers. O-places are like rusty saws, gears without grease, dull knives. They create friction, irritate, chafe, and thwart. They sap human energy rather than release it. The business of business is people, and places that treat people like objects are bad for business. A room without natural light, and with hard metal surfaces, nondescript colors, and bright uniform fluorescent lights is well suited for storing file cabinets, but it contributes nothing to personal motivation or individual productivity. You can recognize an O-place the moment you walk in. Is there a human imprint? If you cannot find one, that office is unlikely to be a good workplace.

MAKING THE OFFICE WORK: CREATING A P-PLACE

How can you make your office environment work better for you? First, you need a way of looking at and thinking about your physical surroundings. What is there? Does what you see serve your purposes? What are the components that might be reorganized, manipulated, removed, shifted, or transformed to create the type of work setting where you work best?

Drawing, writing a report, giving feedback, drafting, doing library research, and just thinking are activities composed of a number of specific behaviors. Each behavior requires some form of physical support. Even a "simple" activity like "drawing" seems straightforward enough. But not when it comes to designing the right office.

One draws, using things like pencils, pen and ink, charcoal, and paint on receptive surfaces like paper, cloth, or wood. Basic supports seem obvious: table or easel, drawing implement. Are these enough? Not according to an artist I talked to. For him "drawing" includes sitting and staring at the uncompleted work; relaxing, getting something to eat, turning on the radio, lying on the bed and letting what he had drawn wash over his consciousness; and it involves concentration, for which he needs privacy and the absence of distraction by others. All these procedures define for him the overall activity "drawing." Only a P-place would provide the full range of supports he needs to draw creatively.

The same kind of simple workstyle analysis can be done for almost any kind of activity you do. You may be surprised to find that the appropriate supports are more varied and extensive than you thought. Drawing requires not only paper, pencil, and surface, but couch, refrigerator, radio, and privacy. How many offices do you know that provide such supports? Yours can—in direct and indirect ways, once you define for yourself exactly what you need. If you read all day, it may be something as simple as a stand that holds your book at a comfortable angle on your desk. If you deal with clients in stressful situations, it may mean an easy chair or small sofa that you can catnap on during lunch hour so that you are refreshed for your afternoon appointments.

A PERSONAL INVENTORY

What do you need from your office? A good place to start to answer that question is with a personal self-appraisal. What are your strengths and weaknesses in relation to different kinds of behavior? My own boss sits at a desk from behind which he can look through his door into a hallway with three administrative offices opening out from it. The hall area is an activity generator. People are constantly walking in and out, visiting with the secretaries, dropping off papers, and so on. Yet I am amazed when I walk into that corridor and glance into his office. He rarely looks up. One of his strengths is his ability to concentrate. He can maintain an "open-door policy" without losing work efficiency because he knows that he can also close the door when he needs to have total concentration or a confidential chat.

If you are easily distracted by others' voices and movements, placing your desk so that you sit facing a busy hallway does not make sense. If you are the kind of person who needs people contact to maintain your motivation and involvement, you might want to make sure that you circulate out several times a day. Placing a small coffeepot in your office can act as an "activity generator" that pulls co-workers into your office. Your office should strengthen those areas where you feel that you are weak.

In thinking about your own strengths and weaknesses, and which behaviors you feel need to be reinforced by environmental support, also think about areas where you are so strong that you may be dysfunctional. I talked with an attorney in a major law firm who stood 6 feet 10

WHAT IS YOUR EQ (ENVIRONMENTAL QUOTIENT)?

Your office is a tool that is essential to doing your best job—as important a tool as a typewriter or calculator or the right business suit. But is it doing all for you that it could? Find out how proficient you are in understanding your office needs.

True or False

_____ 1. A desk facing the door communicates authority.

_____ 2. A messy office shows that you are a hard worker.

_____ 3. Personal objects belong at home.

_____ 4. Some offices just are not worth trying to change.

_____ 5. A good client-centered office should look very bland.

_____ 6. Administrative offices should maximize access to information.

_____ 7. Informal seating arrangements (e.g., couches) are more effective than formal ones (desk and chair and visitors' seating).

_____ 8. Beauty is more important than efficiency in creative workspaces like an artist's studio or a writer's office.

_____ 9. Privacy can reduce effectiveness.

_____10. A square conference table is better than a round one.

Answers on following page.

Scoring: 10 correct: Superb. You know how to use your office to its fullest potential. 7–9 correct: Excellent. You have a good feel for office design, but you need to keep building on it. 6 or fewer: Good but not good enough. Your office is probably working against you.

Answers

1. True. Facing outward gives you a managerial stance. It conveys that you are concerned and accessible.

2. False. A messy office shows only that you are messy and do not care about what the people visiting you think of you. Neatness, within reason, communicates control.

3. False. Especially for women, personal objects in the office tell colleagues and superiors that you are important in areas outside the job—in sports, to a family, etc. This is one of the reasons men display photos of a boat or a spouse. Contrary to some current notions, it makes good political sense to show that you are a whole person.

4. False. Your office is a second skin and you are judged as much by its image as by the clothes you wear.

5. True. If the bulk of your business day involves seeing clients, you will want to be discreet about the personal image you project. Simply because you will want to be all things to all people, you will not want yourself typecast in a certain mode.

6. True. These offices are paper kingdoms, and proper storage means that you will need efficient access to information. And yes, even boxes of files can be made beautiful.

7. False. In formal arrangements, the impression you give is let's-get-down-to-business. Even casual conversations in this setting do more for your image than a feet-on-the desk atmosphere.

8. False. Beauty *is* efficiency in creative workspaces—as a source of inspiration.

9. True. "Closed doors give me the willies," said Joseph Heller's hero in *Something Happened*. Most people need both privacy and people contact—to exchange ideas and to socialize with. It is possible to design yourself private time and space—carefully.

10. True. The beauty of a square or oblong conference table is that it creates distinct boundaries between people. Moreover, such a table permits you to take a "power position" around it by allowing you to face the most powerful person in the meeting. Making eye contact with that person will make you seem to others a figure to be reckoned with.

inches tall and weighed 241 pounds. His intimidating size was reinforced by a very formal personal manner. He was justifiably concerned (and also proud) that he might be overly intimidating to colleagues and clients alike. As a result, when he was given the opportunity to completely design the interior of his own private office, he decided to make it as informal as possible. Mexican tiles and rugs grace the floors, a sofa and soft chairs provide seating, and a small unimposing table serves as a desk. To his delight and amazement several partners in the firm now ask to meet in his office rather than to go to one of the available conference rooms or to their own offices. He relishes the fact that his colleagues are always telling him how much they like his office and what a wonderful job he has done with it. He has very effectively used his surroundings to reveal other sides of his personality, and increased his own satisfaction and relations with others as well.

YOUR OFFICE VS. YOUR POTENTIAL OFFICE

Again and again in visiting different organizations I find that people treat their surroundings as though these surroundings were carved from granite. True, walls, windows, and in many cases, basic furniture and colors may be beyond your control. But even in these situations there are things that you can do. You can rearrange furniture and use it in different ways, bringing in some of your own equipment, decorations, and furniture to lend intimacy to the most institutional setting. Plants make a dreary office come alive and contribute oxygen to stale air. A "white noise" machine to mask disturbing sounds can provide a form of privacy—without offending anybody as a closed door might. Personal storage systems can add beauty and help you create order from chaos. I am continually amazed as I travel around the country talking to lawyers, architects, bankers, executives, professors, and all manner of intelligent people that many of them really think that they cannot alter their offices. They can describe what parts of the office they use, what parts cause problems, and what parts they wish could be changed; but they are often unaware of how they might change the office environment so that it is an asset rather than a liability.

I recently talked with a young attorney in a prestigious law firm who complained about being distracted every time he looked into a hall through a glass wall that separated his office from the corridor. He sat behind his desk facing the corridor. Why? That was the way it was when he moved in! I asked him why he did not move his desk. His first reaction was that it was not possible. Then he laughed nervously and admitted that he did not really know that. He thought that might be the case, and so had not even tried to move the desk. He had created a pseudo-fixed space; he treated the flexible as inflexible.

We create our own surroundings by acting on, and failing to take advantage of, its potentials. Every environment provides opportunities to be used in different ways and at different times. Furniture and equipment can be taken in and out, pictures can be hung on the wall or taken down from it, walls can be painted. This attorney was describing his *effective* environment, the one he happens to make use of. There is a whole other environment, the *potential* environment, which offers so many opportunities that may be ignored.

There are restrictions on what you can do, to be sure. Some of these are formal: written rules and regulations, and the limitations of the space and furnishings themselves. Many more are informal. They are known and enforced through the local office "culture." Our colleagues quickly socialize us into what is acceptable and what is "out of bounds." Frowns, raised eyebrows, a well-placed word or phrase do the trick. But on top of these real restrictions we manage to create our own. You need to more effectively exploit your office's potential. But how?

To make your office work for you, you are going to have to become experimental and playful. Don't worry about looking silly or appearing eccentric or egocentric. If colleagues interpret a concern with your physical

IMPOSSIBLE TO CHANGE?

This is a potential environment. Even what seems like the most tightly constrained workspace can be changed so that it is right for you. The office as it is arranged now serves a few administrative purposes. The long, continuous work surface is ideal for spreading out work, and there is plenty of storage space. However, it would not be comfortable to meet with clients or to hold small meetings here because of the furniture arrangement. With the door open, you could be easily distracted by people passing by in the hall.

What is different in this office? The desk has been flipped to provide an extremely efficient L-shaped work surface. Even if the office culture requires you to keep your door open, you can turn your back to the door when you need concentration privacy.

Here both the desk and work table have been flipped to allow for client-centered activities. The table is a strong barrier, but for male-female interaction it may be a welcome boundary line. A woman sitting behind such a table will convey a greater sense of authority than if she were sitting in any other position. The desk minimizes visual distractions and maximizes privacy when you are working alone.

The table remains flipped here, but the desk is returned to its original position. The outside world is cut off by the table. Inviting visitors to enter the "inner circle" communicates a high level of friendship that can help set a positive tone for meetings. You cannot turn your back to the world when you are at the desk, but the table serving as a barrier reminds others of your need for privacy.

For the first time something old (the table) has been removed
and something new (the coffee table) has been added to the
office. The room now supports more informal and democratic
discussions because the round table is less of a barrier than
the rectangular table. Two very distinct work zones have been
created—a social zone (around the coffee table) and a private
work zone where you can turn your back to the world (the
desk).

Each of the preceding changes took one person approximately one minute to make. Even if you discover
that you do not like the new arrangement after living
with it for a while, at worst you have spent (not
wasted!) two minutes of your time trying to become
more productive. It is worth the effort!

surroundings as evidence of an advanced case of status consciousness or wasted energy, realize that when it comes to their own offices, the story is different!

Try low-risk experiments. They often pay off. I recently talked to a woman who is responsible for all in-house publications for a science museum. Lack of storage space was a constant irritation. One day she tried moving her desk around and ended up placing it away from the walls but at an angle to the corners so that the space between it and the wall formed a triangular shape in which she could sit. To her surprise the new arrangement gave her much-needed wall space in her crowded office. Not only was she amazed that it worked, but perhaps even more so that others in the office who had the same problem saw what she had done and followed suit.

The value of a playful attitude toward our surroundings is that with it we can break habitual patterns whose inefficiencies are matched only by the security their familiarity provides. Do you really need a full-size desk? If you used a narrower shelf-like table instead, would you have room for the small conference table you really want? Storage and filing systems are a headache for almost everyone. Try "zoning" your office—creating different areas for different materials and activities. An architect I know has one table for drafting, another for color work, another for writing, another for financial work. The areas in your own office may be only a foot of a credenza or the back of your desk, but try erecting boundaries. These may be physical, in the form of bookends or boxes or wire storage systems, or they may be symbolic: research notes on top of the blue area, marketing reports on top of the red one. If you have two small file cabinets, can they be stacked one on top of the other to create floor space for an easy chair? One ad man was able to fit a beautiful rolltop desk into his office by using a recessed corner that he at first thought was not suitable for anything besides storage.

MULTIPLE LEVELS OF MEANINGS

As you begin to assess your office's potential and how it can support best your own workstyle, think of your office as helping you on three levels:

- Pragmatic
- Symbolic
- Catalytic.

The Pragmatic Level

You need a desk for writing, a chair for sitting, walls for privacy, shelves and cabinets for storage. These are pragmatic concerns. When your customers' or clients' files form a city-like block of miniature high-rise towers on your desk, you know you have storage problems. The first thought is for more file cabinets, shelving, or—increasingly—access to electronic file systems. But our criteria for selecting a particular chair, shelving system, or set of file cabinets goes beyond mere efficiency. There are a thousand different kinds of desk lamps, chairs, and shelves. Pragmatically, in terms of their utility and efficiency, they may be virtually indistinguishable. So we look for additional distinguishing factors, and these are typically symbolic in nature. Desks, chairs, and storage systems that do not do the job efficiently do not make sense. But neither do equipment and furniture that ignore your more subtle, but equally important, need for meaningful symbolic identification with your physical surroundings.

The Symbolic Level

The way you select and arrange your physical surroundings says something about who you are, what your intentions are, with whom you associate, and what you value and dislike. The meaning of the silent messages your office sends are not always positive, especially if you have to live with desks, chairs, colors, and lights selected by others mainly for their low cost or other narrowly defined efficiencies. Bringing plants, posters, or a favorite desk chair or lamp into your office is an excellent way of creating a workspace that meets your needs on multiple symbolic levels.

The attorney who designed his office around a Mexican motif could have designed his office with gray carpet, walnut paneling, and leather chairs. But his design decisions were largely intended to be symbolic. He wanted people to see him in a different light. He used his office to create a contrary set of impressions about who he was and how he wanted to interact with others.

David Watkins is a TV producer who makes educational films within a university setting. He set himself off from his academic colleagues by furnishing his office with sleek chrome and glass furniture. Basically his office has the same kinds of furniture as most professors offices: desk, bookshelves, desk lamp, chairs for visitors. But symbolically, it is set apart. It, too, works at more than one level.

The Catalytic Level

Third, your office can act as a catalyst that triggers a whole series of linked events and behaviors. A long conference table with chairs lined up and down each side, with the president sitting at the head of the table, is a poor arrangement for a free exchange of ideas. If you sit toward the middle you will participate less than people sitting closer to the president or directly opposite him or her. A long conference table may hinder interaction, and feedback may not be aired. Some individuals may feel that they did not (or were not encouraged to) contribute in a way that they would have liked. Their own satisfaction and sense of involvement will diminish, and their commitments to the "group's" decisions may be minimal. A chain of events has been set in motion that weakens the communication process. Such a chain of events can be started by as innocent a habit as whether you deal with people from behind a desk or at a sofa; or whether your chair is three inches higher than theirs.

Pinpointing the trigger event in a long chain of events is difficult. People are more likely to attribute others' (and often their own) feelings of isolation or dissatisfaction to character defects rather than to environmental defects. To some extent skepticism about the effect of physical surroundings on behavior is justified. It is true that the conference table or room did not cause Bill or

Mary to remain silent, but it may have reinforced shyness when it should have supported assertiveness. We tend to underestimate the physical settings' contribution to successful job performance because we look at only how it supports behavior at a single point in time, and in a direct or pragmatic sense. The environment often operates more subtly.

Most important to using your office as a catalytic tool is realizing that your space is only a part of the whole office. It helps to know what its limitations are. You will not want every meeting to be held on your home turf, believe it or not. Neutral or backstage spaces are crucial—if you can demonstrate the same comfort in them as you do in your office.

Job success and promotion, for example, are only partly based on good performance. They are also based on those who make job advancement decisions knowing what you have done, why, and how. Promotion decisions are based partly on "goodness of fit" assessments: "Bill really belongs here." "Mary isn't our type." We cannot make these types of decisions without context, and informal interaction in a variety of situations is an important stage for filling in context. For example, a large law firm in Washington, D.C. recently had a new office facility designed for it. Recognizing the value of the opportunity for partners and associates to get to know each other in less formal surroundings than their private offices and conference rooms, a special room had been designed to serve essentially as a "living room." Partners and associates were encouraged to gather at the end of a long day for a drink and some informal discussions about the day's events, work going on in the office, and simply to get to know each other. I asked a young attorney in this office if she often went to the "garden room" and whether she felt it important to go. The opportunity to meet partners, discuss cases, and unwind was imporant, she felt, and as a woman she appreciated access in a clublike atmosphere to men at the top. But she rarely took advantage of the garden room. She felt that it did not make much difference. Later the same day, I mentioned this woman's name to some of the partners. None of them had heard of her. They were sure that I had become confused and was talking about either a secretary or someone who had not been in the firm for more than two or three weeks. She had been in the firm for over nine months.

Whether she will eventually be promoted on up the ladder to partner is difficult to know. But I would hazard a guess that if she cannot make herself known to a wide range of partners in the firm via use of the seemingly unimportant social gathering—actually a backstage work area—her chances will be poor. The environment here is actually providing an opportunity to this attorney to make the kinds of contacts that she needs to move up.

Ask youself whether you derive from your office all you can—on each of these three levels. If your office is largely pragmatic, you will have lost a tremendous opportunity to make it announce success. Yet if it is all image, the image will seem insincere and shallow if your actual function is not apparent. You need to build on both levels and on the catalytic level as well, wherein your workspace can motivate and help make you "fit." In the following chapters are the blueprints for using your office to gain status, power, and privacy.

PART TWO

Tools of the Trade

CHAPTER TWO

Status

Status. It will not go away. We all want recognition—
for outstanding achievement, for long service, and for
just being ourselves. Yet because an important part of
our lives is defined by our jobs, we are hungriest for
recognition in the workplace—precisely where it is the
most elusive.

Since the folks responsible for back-patting realize
that most of us want recognition in public as well as in
private, when we are rewarded it is often with status
changes in our physical surroundings: larger offices,
wider views, better carpeting, a bigger desk, a stainless-
steel ashtray, a plaque, a corner office, the top floor.

Adequate space, storage, and privacy, as well as comfortable chairs and good lighting, are at the very core of
worker satisfaction and productivity. For just these reasons such valuable environmental resources are not the
best status cues. Think of it! Rewarding achievement
with space or privacy or comfort is like giving a track star
a piece of the track instead of a trophy. Status is symbolic. It makes sense to reward it symbolically and
publicly.

Jobs where no one has a permanent office show how status can be recognized symbolically without using productive resources like office size or privacy. Nurses and generals win status cues with insignias: ribbons on the chest and in the cap and different kinds and colors of caps and uniforms. Professions that are not set in offices have had to invent new ways of marking status distinctions. What good is a bigger tent on the front line? The irony, as psychologist Lawrence Williams points out, is that the higher the position and the larger the office, the less time the occupant tends to spend in that office. The boss is more likely traveling around the country, working at home, or meeting clients in the conference room or restaurant, while the middle-level manager and the subordinates are locked into their small and poorly furnished offices.

CAN YOUR IMAGE LIVE UP TO YOUR ABILITY?

The answer is yes—in spite of the fact that virtually all large organizations have detailed space standards. These take the form of elaborate rules specifying the amount of space and number, type, and quality of furnishings to which individuals at a given level in the pecking order are entitled. As manager you might get 350-400 square feet, a partition that goes to the ceiling, a door to the office, executive furniture, carpeting, and a table with eight chairs. Your assistant may get only 108 square feet, a six-foot-high partition, no door, and a name plate that states his or her operation and function.

The promise of a bigger and better office may sometimes motivate "stars" on their way up, but more often it is likely to be a constant irritant. Progressive organizations realize this and are beginning to develop creative space standards that preserve status without undermining individual productivity.

At Austeel, a Japanese-owned mini-steel mill in Auburn, New York, an attempt has been made to raise everyone's status. Every office in the administration building is identical, with only one exception. The secretary's office at the end of the hall is larger than the company president's! Space standard's only saving grace is that you know that you are not being treated any worse than the next guy. Yet not even these restrictions have to stand in your way.

The entire office of Arnold and Porter, attorneys, for example, attacked status in an even more innovative way. All employees selected their own offices in a new building. Order of selection was based on seniority. The most senior partner picked his office first and then on down to the newest associate. The unusual twist was that the office was designed intentionally to undermine the ability of an outsider to come in and immediately assess an employee's status on the basis of office size or location. Rather than having a senior partner's office ten times the size and the plushness of the most junior associate's office, the whole range of office sizes was deliberately compressed so that the "small" offices were about as large as the "big" offices.

To recreate some of the sense of the small Georgian residence in which the law firm had been located when

GUESS WHICH ONE IS THE COMPANY PRESIDENT *Status does not have to be expressed in office size or the quality of furnishings. Who is the President? The offices of all the executives are identical in size. The largest individual office is occupied by a secretary.*

it was much smaller, the designers were also directed to create different-shaped offices, and told not to piggyback the best features of offices. The biggest offices do not have the best views, nor are the smallest offices located in dark recesses of the interior. The lawyers' status is not reflected in the size of an office or its location. In fact, in some cases senior partners ended up with smaller offices than associates.

One partner chose a small office with high ceilings over a larger office with lower ceilings. Another preferred being able to see sky and nondescript buildings rather than a view of interesting buildings. Still another chose an odd-shaped office because he wanted something different. Offices indicated more what their occupants valued than who they were in the office pecking order.

By no means are status cues consigned to the dustbin. In fact, they are all pervasive, but members bask in them as a collectivity. The entire office says "top drawer" through fine woods, beautiful carpets and furnishings, and heavy brass fittings. Status is also preserved in other ways. Senior partners receive higher salaries. They choose the best cases and assign them to their friends and protégés. They make the major decisions in meetings. By their age and experience they daily let others know where they stand in the pecking order. Others can tell who they are in a personal sense through the way each designed his or her own office.

Once they had selected the offices they wanted on the basis of seniority, the attorneys were permitted to design their own offices as they pleased. The results are startling, as the accompanying photographs indicate. Each of the partners is an individual, and his or her office shows it. One can walk from the traditional dark wood-paneled office with leather chairs and heavy air of Old English to a living room-like office finished with bright-colored fabrics and colorful Mexican rugs and tiles. There is no uniformity here. Does it work?

Informal conversations with several partners and associates say "yes." Junior associates have larger and better appointed offices than they might have in other firms. This is significant since large firms like Arnold and Porter often have difficulty attracting the most outstanding young attorneys, who often prefer smaller offices where they can make a bigger splash. Several senior partners responsible for recruiting and hiring young attorneys felt that the elegant surroundings and egalitarian office sizes contributed to their ability to attract the very best young attorneys. Not one of the attorneys I interviewed felt that the differences in personal style revealed in the individual offices worked to the detriment of the attorneys vis-à-vis each other. All felt that the opportunity to design their own offices contributed very positively to their own satisfaction and ability to work effectively.

If you do not have the luck to work for a relatively enlightened firm, what can you do? Do not panic. Remember that your individual needs for recognition are (or should be) as important to the company as they are to you. The last thing you want to do is start by saying that you want more recognition or status. Particularly in fields like engineering and banking, that is a good

Tools of the Trade

The occupants of these four different offices all work for the same firm. Yet the arrangement and style of the furnishings and decorations set an individual, distinctive tone for each office. The occupant's personality emerges, making each office a P-Place.

strategy for being labeled a lazy, egocentric, nonprofessional malcontent and troublemaker. The premise, of course, is that really productive people are not concerned about such trivial things as status and office layout because they are so busy grinding out the work. Status is not the key. Recognition is, and particularly the recognition of individual differences that allow you to work the most effectively.

ACHIEVING RECOGNITION: YOUR OWN STAMP OF STATUS

Right now there is status hidden in your office surroundings, in the decor, coverings, and type of furnishings, and in the way these are arranged and the degree of privacy they provide. Uncovering the status symbols for all to see is not difficult.

First, think about getting together with your co-workers and cooperatively selecting and organizing your surroundings to enhance your status as a group. Differences of opinion will float to the surface, but the dissension will occur in a positive context. The more of you that cooperate, the more talent and energy (and possibly money) you can marshall to improve your shared workspace. Considering how hard it is for people to work in groups, the fact that you were even able to help initiate and see through a successful collective action will enhance your personal and organizational status. Your office environment becomes a communication medium through which you can send some positive messages about abilities of yours that otherwise have no outlet.

Status

At the Washington law firm of Arnold and Porter, status surroundings are shared. All the public spaces are of the highest quality, and the impact benefits all who work there, regardless of their place in the office pecking order.

If you are offered the opportunity to participate in designing some aspect of your office, take it. You benefit in three ways. First, your participation demonstrates a commitment to the firm and a willingness to become involved. Second, it gives you a forum, as I have noted above, for demonstrating skills that may lead to your being viewed in a new light, and thus to promotions and new assignments. Third, you may be able to create an image and work environment that genuinely reflects who you are or want to be.

Being able to paint your own equipment or to decorate your office the way you like is not going to compensate for other negative work practices, or for work that you cannot see as having any value in its own right, but it can enhance your status by allowing you to project an individual and/or collective image that reinforces your own self-worth and communicates it to others. People respond to the images you project. If clothing is a second layer of skin, your office environment is a third, and you need to dress it (and you) for success.

IN STATUS, LESS IS MORE

Being a manager entails a special kind of status. You are set apart from others by the nature of activities, and to some extent by the need to have your special decision-making powers reinforced. You do not need the biggest office and the best view to be acknowledged in this role. Sometimes these perquisites can work against you.

Robert Sommer is one of the most creative people I know. When he was given a managerial role in the psychology department at the University of California, he thought of himself as the "phantom chairman." With his promotion he was expected to move from his large, pleasant office on the second floor. He decided, instead, to remain in his own office. The chairperson's office became the department lounge and coffee room. Why did he shun such a visible symbol of having "made it"? For a good reason.

Sommer was not interested in having to greet every visitor to the department, or in being so accessible that people would pass the smallest decisions over his desk. He wanted to remain productive, to write and do research. Sommer's organization of space and therefore people also left him free to really "manage": to think about the larger questions of direction, purpose, goals, and objectives—without sacrificing activities he loved.

Status comes in different packages. Choosing between one form and another can be difficult, especially when both offer advantages and disadvantages. When he first started his small ad agency, one advertising executive with whom I talked made his office command central. It was the pivot point around which swirled employees and clients alike. Here, less privacy was more status. After many years, the central location made it too easy for employees to check with him and ask his opinions. As an innovative and effective manager, part of his goal is to increase the decision-making effectiveness of those working for him. Removing his office location from its command position made him less central but more private. By becoming less visible he became more effective.

Using your office to highlight your special position as manager may be personally gratifying but organizationally dysfunctional. Clients want to deal with top people. They do not want second best. If they go into a firm, see large distinctions in offices, and are then shepherded to what looks like the second stringers' offices, they may feel shortchanged. Greater uniformity among the offices indicates to outsiders that everyone in the firm is important. Being shown into the third office on the right has no less meaning than being shown to one that is close to the door. Not only does this spread the workload more evenly and take advantage of everyone's talent, but it frees the energy of the manager from meetings and interactions that detract from time that could be more productively spent elsewhere.

So how can status recognition be marked? With a larger desk, a little more space around the desk and storage cabinets, the use of contrasting color, and even the simplest device of all: a sign saying "Manager"! Adding a low platform or partial enclosure to one corner of the office where you might arrange a seating area gives you a necessary distinctiveness but not a dysfunctional one. Having one's own CRT or other high-tech equipment would also set you off from the rest of the herd. These are all visible distinctions, but none of them affects other office functions.

Within an organization, there is generally little ambiguity about who really has the power, and who has only the furniture. In looking at status tools, or the building blocks of status, keep in mind that much of what we call status is really related to personal recognition and identity rather than to power per se. Even in the most restrictive organizations, there is still much you can do to enhance your own status and personal recognition.

PERSONAL STATUS TOOLS

Personal momentos

A recent book on success strategies for women in business caution that personal momentos appear only on the retiree's desk. But is this so? Does it make sense to deliberately mask one's personal identity in a business situation? Based on visits to small and large businesses all over the country, the answer is a resounding "no."

In office after office I find shelves lined with old school athletic pictures, family photos, achievement awards, examples of hobbies like photography, and almost every other conceiveable form of personal momento. When you walk into such offices you know at once that the person occupying it is saying, "Welcome to my office. This is me." The idea that personal recognition in the work environment should be reserved for senior statesmen ignores the tremendous need for personal recognition I discussed earlier. You should not throw anything and everything onto your walls, but the range of acceptable items is very large.

If you are a woman, and women's status within your organization is still shaky, you should use care in placing

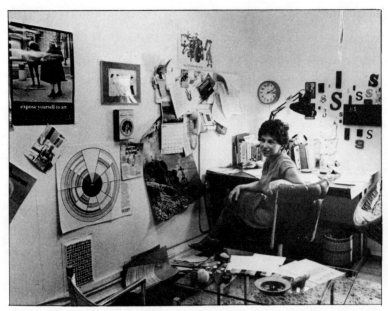

Sandy Gurowitz's own creative work hangs on her walls. It expresses all the attributes important to a creative copy writer: inventiveness, humor, individuality, and productivity.

personal momentos in your office, but there is no need to avoid their use entirely. In fact, judicious use of personal momentos may convey a sense of confidence in your own identity and status rather than undermining it, as would the attempt to become Ms. or Mr. Anonymous. There are a number of acceptable categories of personal momentos.

Athletic Momentos

Participation and achievement in athletics continue to be a valued clue to everything from one's leadership ability to physical prowess and personality. Depending upon the particular sport, participation also says something about one's class and life style. Although we often think of sports as being men's special province, this area is changing rapidly. There are a number of different athletic endeavors that enhance, rather than undermine, women's status in the office. Sports like swimming, tennis, golf, polo, gymnastics, fencing, riding, rowing, and track are not only practiced by both men and women, but are generally viewed as high-status sports. Pictures of yourself in action, of your team, and pieces of equipment that are interesting art objects in themselves all can take their place in the office without embarrassment or apology. They will contribute to your own sense of who you are, as well as help others quickly get a sense of the person with whom they are interacting. The way in which such momentos can be used as part of the social influence process is discussed in the next chapter.

Family Photographs

There is some feeling that women who display family pictures or a five-year-old son's painting will have their behavior construed more negatively than men who display the same sort of objects. The concern is that women will be seen as people who are not really committed to work, while men will be viewed as stable "family men." My own feeling is that to be effective people need to work in environments they find to be personally comfortable. For a vast number of people this means having reminders of their family around to let others know that they have other valued identities. It does not mean that you have to plaster all your four-year-old's finger paintings everywhere on the wall, however. Pictures in frames convey a greater sense of order and class than unframed and torn pieces of paper. A family photo facing you, and located on your desktop or a nearby shelf or credenza, is a discreet way of communicating these personal identities. The fact that you are willing to acknowledge your family members and your multiple roles can convey that you have enough confidence in yourself to be able to display such objects without apology or embarrassment.

I have also seen pictures not only of immediate family members, or even living ones, but of grandparents and other relatives. Americans have a fascination with history, and these kinds of historical family photographs are a way of connecting your own personal family history and identity to longer historical traditions. Particularly when they include images of older housing, cars, towns, or ways of life, these photographs can be both fascinating and informative. A variation on this theme is the possibility of bringing in photographs or small busts of famous historical figures whom you particularly enjoy and whose words or deeds you value. One director of a small ad agency I know has his personal office and the conference room adorned with Lincoln memorabilia. Everything from photographs and small sculptures to framed sayings adorn the walls and tables. He is able to identify himself with a revered figure in American history, to associate some of his characteristics with Lincoln's, and to provide a focal point for newcomers to his office that can put them at ease and start conversation smoothly rolling.

Hobbies

Although you want to convey to others that you are a hard worker, you also want to convey that you are multidimensional. Displays of hobbies let you communicate another side of your personality. Depending upon what they are, these hobbies may also contribute to your work image because they say something about your creativity, your intelligence, or your organizational abilities.

Framed photographs you have taken are always appropriate. They say not only something about you as a photographer, but their subject matter tells something about your other interests. Coin and stamp collections or your favorite collection of butterflies are fascinating to most people. If you have built a special piece of furniture or done a particularly nice painting, these also can contribute in positive ways to your personal recognition and status within the office. These kinds of hobbies actually enhance your work image because they say something positive about your creativity, your astuteness as a collector, and your technical skill.

Humor

Humor is tricky. Self-deprecating humor is generally safer than humor bought at the expense of others' values and personal foibles. Political humor is often frowned upon in organizations, unless it supports what is known to be the bosses' or board of directors' own political leanings. Cartoons or books that poke fun at the world of business in general are more likely to be accepted. Even more acceptable is humor grounded in life's daily oddities, or simple unexpected events and actions. Pictures of people in humorous juxtaposition to each other or to various objects say something about your sense of humor without poking fun at anyone. One person who works with the handicapped has a lifesize plastic model sitting in a wheelchair looking at a report on handicapped accessibility. People appreciate the humor and also learn something about his professional interests. The more subtle and dry your humor, the higher its, and your, status will be. Canned jokes add less to your prestige than the ability to spin off one-liners in the heat of verbal sparring with your colleagues.

THE OFFICE ENVIRONMENT

Even in a tightly controlled office situation you can use status cues that are more subtle than those already mentioned, but that still have bite.

Signs

The most obvious, but often overlooked, way of communicating status is through signs. Signs are explicit, and depending upon the materials used, they can convey not only explicit information like "manager," but also something about the organization and the individual. Black presstype, of the sort that architects use routinely in their presentations, is easy to apply and inexpensive, and conveys an image of quality and authority if you use something like a standard Helvetica typeface, which is bold, simple, and authoritative. Custom-made signs, available at most stationery and office-supply stores as well as at trophy stores, can produce your name and title in brass, steel, plastic, wood, or whatever material you want. These can go on your door, partition, or desk.

Location

Traditionally, the corner office with windows on two sides indicates high status. If you have some control over location, however, there are other possibilities. Centrality—locating yourself so that you are visible to everyone—can be a status symbol. You become the "command center" and the person to whom others look for guidance.

Since the purpose of status cues for authority is to distinguish oneself from others, these kinds of largely symbolic devices can be very useful without wasting the scarce resources of space and enclosure that might be better used to meet the work needs of all persons in the organization. The real point is that status cues for authority must in some way make you stand out from others in the office. If everyone is out front, then being in the back may make sense. If everyone is in the back, being up front may make sense.

Position Within the Office

Even within your office, the position of your desk may help communicate your authority status. A desk directly facing the door, at which you sit so that you are visible from the entrance to your office, communicates a sense of authority that is different from that of the person whose desk is placed against the wall in a corner of the office. The openness of the desk to outsiders communicates that part of your responsibility is meeting with other people and dealing with their concerns. Placing your desk so that your back faces the door says that you do not have much responsibility for dealing with people, which is a primary activity we associate with high-status managers. A desk placed against a wall so that it is perpendicular to the door communicates accessibility without being intimidating.

Office Size

Generally, the larger the office, the more we associate it with high status. The same is true with enclosure. The person whose office walls go from the floor to the ceiling is generally assumed to have a higher status than the person whose office walls go from the floor to his or her waist. As I have already argued, many elements like walls and barriers are better used to enhance activities that need privacy and work concentration, thereby contributing directly to effectiveness. It is also possible to think of trade-offs in environmental elements. Having a small but centrally located office may be a better indicator of authority status than a very large office located backstage. Similarly, a smaller office with an excellent view may convey status effectively.

Lighting

The person who suffers under a blanket of fluorescent lights seems to have less authority than the person with the individual flexible lamp or the recessed lighting under a workstation counter. Individual light sources that provide the opportunity to create flexible lighting suited for particular tasks are generally associated with higher status. Warm-toned and diffuse fluorescent lighting that is nicely framed is a good compromise, especially where energy concerns are high.

You may be able to exercise more control over lighting status cues than those in other areas. You are less likely to be prohibited from bringing in a personal lamp than a Persian carpet. Not only the type of light but the style of lamp will also contribute to your status. It is hard to go wrong with the traditional flexible lamps, which come in a variety of colors and which can attach directly to the desk or be placed in a solid base. Black or white will convey a greater sense of professionalism because they are somewhat muted and understated. Bright colors convey more creativity and spontaneity. A small antique lamp, like the ones that have a green opaque shade over a brass base, can also provide subtle and soft lighting and at the same time convey a sense of individuality.

Colors

Colors, like materials and finishes, should be more understated than flashy. They should be rich in tone but subdued in nature. They can be bright but not gaudy. Bright yellow, flaming pink, purple, fire-engine red, lime green, or turquoise may be your favorite colors, but a lot of people hate them; they are not associated with someone on the way up or already there. Solids or relatively subdued patterns are likely to be more acceptable than busy patterns. White walls cannot be beat, but painting one wall as an accent wall a relatively bright color—or a more subdued color like a chocolate brown or dark blue—will add life to a room without becoming overpowering. Still, if bright colors are your medium, small brightly colored objects like lamps, pencil holders, and wall hangings add zest to a bland office without making a trumpet-like blast that may alienate your co-workers or clients.

Equipment and Toys

Whatever is the latest—whether it is the smallest, the fastest, the loudest, or the most complex—is associated with high status. And do not forget toys. The beauty of toys is that they are often miniature art objects in themselves, and can say a great deal about you. Are you creative, playful, wealthy, smart? An exquisite chess set on top of a credenza says something very different than a stereo system or hand-carved Mexican spinning top. Toys will probably contribute more to personal recogni-

Shelves filled with antique dental equipment and supplies are a delightful way of creating visual interest and communicating this professional's values—the appreciation of dental history and progress. The display also indicates that this dentist is well-established and settled, certainly not a newcomer.

tion and identity than to any authority status, although we tend to associate such conspicuously nonwork items with a person secure in his or her identity.

Awards

The business world is sensitive to people's need to have their achievement documented and visible. Awards, plaques, certificates, and trophies are routinely handed out for everything from making the most sales during the last month to attending a computer work-

Photographs showing you with famous people are strong status cues, and may also serve as ice-breakers: "How did you meet President Kennedy?" "Well, I was . . ."

shop. Place these on your walls. They are one of the most acceptable ways of conveying what you have done, what you have learned, and where you have been. Special photographs of you with particular persons or particular places are also effective. It is very impressive to walk into an office and see on the wall a photograph of its occupant talking casually with John F. Kennedy or Lyndon Johnson. You immediately get the sense that you are in the presence of someone important.

Your use of a combination of these kinds of status and recognition cues will not guarantee your becoming the chairman of the board. But at the very least these cues will help you feel more comfortable in your own work-place, and therefore more effective. As you will see in the next chapter, the value of status cues also lies in their contribution to your social influence in the organization. In subtle ways they help structure communication and interaction and contribute to direct impressions of who and what you are.

No office will really work if these different kinds of status considerations—each centered on satisfying a different form of recognition—are not accommodated and integrated into every office design. P-places balance these functions. O-places tend to focus on only one or two, and usually shortchange the need for personal recognition. Status cannot be designed out. Used appropriately, it can promote everyone's effectiveness.

CHAPTER THREE

Privacy

If you are not bothered by a lack of privacy at work, you are either sitting close to the top of the pyramid in an unusual office, or you have a great capacity for screening out distractions. But for most people who work in offices, privacy is a major issue. As one man in a study of partitioned modular office complained, "There are constant interruptions, and everything you say is overheard, which means you can't talk to an employer about poor performance unless you parade him or her into a conference room, and then everybody can see what's happening." Or as another commented, "Only courtesy and general amiability of the staff prevent this from being an absolute snake pit. Seated at a desk in a cubicle, one is visually isolated but continually assaulted by distracting noise—exactly the reverse of my preferred workstyle."

Most of us need some time and space that we can control: a place to collect our thoughts, generate an advertising campaign, recharge our batteries, let our hair down, daydream. We need a place to grouse and reconsider, to lick wounds, to gossip, and to concentrate. The difference between having privacy and only dreaming about it is the difference between headaches and health, high energy and lethargy, sociability and withdrawal. The essence of privacy is the control of information flow.

INPUT/OUTPUT: GAINING PRIVACY CONTROL

Most of us think about privacy in terms of other people bothering us. But this is only half the matter. In fact, you need privacy just as much so that you do not bother or embarrass others. Privacy therefore is both an *input* problem—distracting noise, sights, and movement that others create and that disturb or interrupt us—and an *output* problem—noise, activities, and interaction that we generate and that we do not want others to observe or monitor. Information flow is the issue: what we reveal of ourselves and learn about others.

As psychologist Irwin Altman has put it, privacy is essentially a process of setting up boundaries. We are constantly striving to strike a balance between the amount and type of interaction we have with others, and the type and amount we want to have with others. Too much privacy and we experience *isolation;* too little and we experience *crowding* and *stress*. Since the critical component of privacy is information flow, crowding is not necessarily related to density, that is, the number of other warm bodies sharing the space. Two people exchanging office gossip in a 450-square-foot space may feel "crowded" if their conversation can be overheard by someone on the other side of a partition. At the core of privacy is control: the ability to regulate information.

TYPES OF PRIVACY: THE THREE Cs

Privacy needs are individual and dynamic. For some people the silence of a library is tormenting. For others, it's a necessary sanctuary. Individuals are different; but in addition, the same person's needs change over time. I do not need the same privacy to write a letter as I do to draft an article. After holing up in my study at home all morning, I want activity and interaction. To accommodate your workstyle, your workplace must offer you these three different types of privacy:

· Communication
· Concentration
· Contemplation

Communication Privacy

You interact with friends and colleagues at work for many different reasons. As a manager you are required to give others feedback on how they are doing, whether their effort is on target or off base, whether it is up to your standards or not. And often there is the need to brainstorm or to test your ideas on others before formalizing them. You also need to communicate with others to start office friendships, and to cement them. Personal relationships provide the backbone of cooperation and trust. Without them, most of us are reluctant to share ideas and information or to pool talents and skills to improve a clinical diagnosis, a legal defense strategy, or an advertising headline. And of course there is gossip. Communication privacy refers to situations in which all of these kinds of information exchanges can occur with a minimum of restrictions.

Communication privacy is important because we do not say the same things to people in private as we do in public. This is especially true for communicating negative information, the hardest kind to talk about under any circumstances. Yet it is often necessary to communicate "bad news" to others, particularly when you evaluate others' performance. The opportunity for privacy in such situations may mean the difference between an accurate and a distorted assessment.

If you have a private office, dealing with such situations is easier, but problems remain. Dave Banfield, the informal "personnel director" of a small insurance agency, notes that "when I call somebody in my office and shut the door, I think I can sense that they are scared or nervous, or they don't understand or don't know what I am going to talk about." Communication privacy will not eliminate such anxieties, but it can help keep them to a manageable level. At least you do not have to worry about publicly embarrassing an employee (or having the employee try to publicly embarrass you or challenge your authority) if you can meet in a private office.

HOW MUCH PRIVACY DO YOU NEED?

Too much privacy can be as dysfunctional as too little. What is your own best workstyle? Answer "Yes" or "No" to the following statements and discover the kind of space that meets your privacy needs.

Yes   No

1. When I work alone, I usually close my door.
2. I have arranged my desk so I can look up without making eye contact with passers-by.
3. I am easily distracted by the conversations of people near me.
4. Autonomy and independence are of overriding importance to me in my work.
5. The presence of others impedes my ability to complete tasks.
6. I do not need to be easily accessible to my co-workers at all times.
7. Casual interaction with others at work is not of great importance to me.
8. I do not rely on co-worker feedback to accomplish my tasks.
9. I do not need to see and hear what my co-workers are doing.
10. I do not socialize with my co-workers during office hours.
11. When I am working on certain tasks, I indicate to others that I do not want to be disturbed.
12. I cannot speak freely when I know others can overhear my conversations.

Scoring

If you answered "Yes":

1–4 times: The office that best matches your privacy needs is a hub. You enjoy being in the center of things. In your work it is crucial that you are accessible to others and that you can interact with them freely. You need to be aware of what is happening around you and to be able to exchange information with co-workers.

5–8 times: Although you need quiet and privacy when you are working on tasks alone, interaction with others is an important priority. You need an office that provides you with seclusion, yet that occasionally gives you access to other people as well.

9–12 times: In order to maximize your effectiveness, your office should be your refuge. You work best alone, away from distractions and the hustle and bustle of office routine. Access to other people is not often important for your work. Quiet and being able to concentrate are major priorities.

How can privacy help you function? The opportunity to exchange feedback in private is valuable both to the person receiving it and the person giving it. Don Ross is a young reporter, new to the trade. The transition from the incessant clatter of the newsroom to the quiet of his boss's office helps him shift gears. "When you leave the newsroom and go into the conference room or an editor's office, there is a very formal attitude you take on. It's almost like a cloistered atmosphere because it's quiet. You don't hear the clattering and it's like going into confession. You take on a very serious, thoughtful attitude when you go into the conference room." Here the critical design element is the contrast in sound and activity levels—the sense of calm in a stormy sea—that the totally enclosed room provides. The change in sounds and activity levels signals the crossing of an invisible psychological boundary and it helps trigger a different mood and attitude.

Without a comfortable place to secure communication privacy you may be less likely to offer confidential feedback as problems begin to evolve. You end up wasting more energy coping with the underlying tension than dealing with the basic problem. Having an office that provides communication privacy, that is used for all kinds of meetings, some occasionally with the door closed, creates the opportunity to invite an employee into the office for emotionally charged discussions without signaling "special events" the way a public march to a conference room often does.

Privacy

The Client's Needs

Privacy is for many people largely an input problem. Other people's noise, movement, and conversation distracts us from our work and makes us less efficient. But for many professionals—lawyers, accountants, therapists, insurance and real estate agents, stockbrokers— the problem is more complex. Privacy is an issue for your client as well as for you. And you are responsible for providing it. The ability to offer your client a sense of privacy may, in fact, be more important to him than to you.

There are many ways of providing privacy. One strategy is to fight noise with noise. In stockbroker Betty Cornish's office conversational cover is made "with the computer coming, and Dow ticker going, and everybody talking." White noise pumped through the ventilation system provides a similar sound cover, as does softly played music. But is masking the sound of conversation sufficient?

John Dieters-Hagen, a partner in a small upstate New York accounting office, explained the value of sound control for communication privacy: "Privacy of the client's financial information is always his foremost consideration, and should as well be our foremost consideration. Generally, if I'm interviewing someone in the office, the door is always closed. It is closed for a variety of reasons. The most important is that the client is usually undergoing a question-and-answer routine: If he is distracted, he may forget what questions he wants to ask or he might lose his train of thought in answering a particular question, and overlook something. Privacy contributes to the fact that the client is in a position to be a lot more open."

Visual Privacy

Visual privacy is also critical whenever sensitive, embarrassing, or ambiguous information is communicated simply by the sight of certain activities or people in public view. Being seen with your boss in the company cafeteria may be an asset, but it may also threaten your colleagues and lead to damaging rumors. Your personal workstyle may also best be kept out of view, especially if it contrasts with your bosses'. Messy workers understand messy workers, and often associate messiness with creativity and spontanity. But people who require order view messy work areas as chaotic and inefficient. They want to see clean surfaces and neat shelves. If you do not work well that way, the visual privacy of an enclosed office may be critical to your bosses' impression of you. You might try to locate your materials out of view in a little-traveled part of the office, or use storage systems with lids and drawers so that the ordered mess of your work activities can be easily shut out of sight at the day's end or on a moment's notice. A rolltop desk is perfect for just this sort of thing.

In some professions, such as psychiatry, communication privacy requires total visual privacy as well as auditory privacy. Because the need for psychiatric help is still viewed by many as a character defect and sign of personal weakness, many patients want to conceal the fact that they are in therapy from people they know. For psychiatrist Christopher Bull this means pulling the curtains across a large picture window that opens onto a charming wooded glen. The problem? A path runs through the glen and near his window. Anybody walking by could casually look in and recognize who was in therapy.

Your ability to provide your client with adequate levels of privacy may make the difference between top-quality and merely acceptable work. This is true, not because of any lack of competence or concern on your part, but rather because the total environmental conditions under which you work are undermining your and your client's effectiveness. Most clients are unaware of how the lack of privacy influences the nature of the information they provide, and thus the quality of help they receive.

What you must be aware of in striving for your own type of appropriate privacy is that your own behavior changes under different kinds of environmental conditions. Like the storyteller in the popular children's book *Twice Upon a Time*, you may believe that "I am what I am," and that you say the same kinds of things under noisy conditions as you do under quiet ones. Yet the contrary is true. Psychological studies repeatedly show that other people's judgments of our own competencies and worth are adversely affected when made in ugly and noisy environments, for example.

Be aware that it is risky to depend upon the client to request privacy. A few will do so, as stockbroker Betty Cornish finds. "The client might say, I would feel better to have this more confidential. Some people are used to having the conditions the way they want them." But more often, Cornish said, people do not ask often for privacy. In any case, you should not expect an outsider to be responsible for structuring your office environment. It can only reflect badly to him on your sense of power and control.

If you do not have a private office, you can still obtain communication privacy. Suggest moving to an unoccupied conference room or getting a cup of coffee in a nearby lounge or restaurant. During off-hours these kinds of places can be very quiet and they are often comfortable. If you cannot leave because you are tied to important equipment, as stockbrokers are to computers, try arranging your furniture to maximize privacy. A useful solution is to face a visitor's chair away from major circulation paths and entrances, and to place it close enough to your own chair so that quiet conversation tones are comfortable and appropriate. A distance of no more than four feet keeps people seated in your own territorial "bubble"—just close enough to feel private and trustful.

The concern for meeting the client's privacy requirements also extends to the handling of records. Many clients do not like the idea that others may accidentally have access to their private information. Keeping clients' files and clients' records out of sight reduces the look of clutter and projects to the client that their information is inaccessible to other clients. If files and forms must be on the desk, you can simply keep them turned over. Or to keep curious co-workers from glancing over appointment calendars or other papers on your desk, place plants near the desk to create a visually pleasant soft barrier. Plants are more of a psychological deterrent than is a harsher barrier like a screen, and they can be more effective for that reason. They do the job without communicating a siege mentality.

Concentration Privacy

Unlike communication privacy, which is both an input and an output problem, concentration privacy is largely an input problem: effectively filtering out unwanted sounds, sights, and activities that distract from what you are doing. Everybody needs different amounts of quiet or inactivity to concentrate. For some people, turning their backs on a busy hallway is all they need to concentrate on the work at hand. For others, closed doors and devices like white-noise machines, which filter out distracting noise, are necessities for a quiet working atmosphere.

There is a danger, however, in putting up too many barriers between you and your co-workers. "Quality time," time to yourself during which you can concentrate without interruption is critical, but so is "quality contact." Fifteen-second encounters on the stairs or in the elevator give a sense of connectedness, and often serve as the trunklines of office gossip (a very important form of professional knowledge). They are indispensable, but they do not substitute for quality contact with colleagues—the opportunity to bang heads together, try out new ideas, test the waters.

The high level of interaction made possible, if not inevitable, by landscaped offices with low partitions may stimulate "communication," but the important question is not "how much" but "what kind." The increased opportunity for informal contact may not increase quality contacts for which more privacy is required, and for which the necessity to schedule a meeting helps create a deadline and the pressure to come to the meeting with an idea well enough developed to present coherently. Many creative people operate well under pressure, but it is the pressure of a deadline rather than that of distractions.

If you want concentration privacy for "quality contact" so that you can meet with someone else without being disrupted, there are a number of things that you can do. Try inviting someone who is leaning over your partition into your office. Moving across the threshold of your entrance creates a different time sense. It says that you are available for a longer period of time. It can also reduce some of the discomfort of trying to talk to someone who is looking down at you. It may be especially useful if the person talking with you is particularly powerful and dominant. Having him or her sit down at the same level equalizes the conversation and can make it more comfortable. Conversations that start in a hallway, on the stairs, or in the elevator can be extended from polite chit-chat to a more serious conversation by inviting the person for a cup of coffee or by finding a place to sit down. Moving to a chair communicates that you are interested and willing to become involved for more than a few seconds.

Contemplation Privacy

In addition to concentration and communication privacy, we also need privacy to attend to ourselves—to reflect on who we are or would like to be, to go over the day's events and make sense of them. Why did I become so defensive when asked that question? Was there some underlying motive in its being asked? Do I need to rethink my strategies for interacting with people, for generating ideas, for how I organize my time? Contemplation privacy allows us to daydream and to completely relax.

Contemplation privacy's contribution to our work is often inadvertent and surprising. This type of privacy enables you to make connections among disparate events, gain new insights into yourself or a problem that you are working on. It allows your mind to flow unrestricted by conscious logic and deliberate plans. It offers time when some of your best ideas emerge. The problem in arranging a workplace is that contemplation privacy occurs best when we are lying down, sitting with our feet propped up on the desk, munching on a sandwich or having a drink, or just falling off to sleep. It is the rare boss, indeed, who could observe one of her or his employees in such activities and not wonder when that employee was going to start "working." The paradox of contemplation or personal privacy is that in many ways it is the foundation of all work effectiveness—yet it seems to be the essence of nonwork. That is why the kinds of activities it involves are often done at home rather than at the "official" workplace.

The strategies described earlier for obtaining visual privacy work well for contemplation privacy as well. You want to get out of view of others, where you can "let down your hair" and do things that would be considered inappropriate, if not embarrassing, were they done in public. To give your colleagues a better set of cues for interpreting what they might otherwise see as nonwork behavior, you might also try using some explicit signaling devices. Putting on the outside of your door or partition a sign that says, "Please don't disturb: writing a report" is very direct. A more subtle one might be sitting with your feet propped up on the desk looking out the window and holding a dictaphone in your hand. The dictaphone is a prop that transforms what appears to be nonwork behavior into work! In some cases, you may want to leave your own office entirely. If you think that others are going to form the wrong impression watching you eat a sandwich in your office at 10:00 A.M., go to the cafeteria. Not only are people less likely to see you, but what you are doing fits the setting. If they see you working with papers spread out on the table, people will immediately understand that you are indeed working and not loafing.

TOOLS OF PRIVACY

Walls

The ultimate privacy tool is a wall. The problem is that walls have shrunk from a brick, plaster, or drywall barrier that went from the floor to the ceiling—providing total visual privacy and generally excellent to passable auditory privacy—to partitions that can be as low as three to four feet high made from wood, particle board, metal, and other materials that may or may not be covered with sound-absorbing materials such as carpet and foam. Top-of-the-line partitions made by companies such as Herman Miller, Knoll, Westinghouse, and others have been designed to mask a given level of sound. Usually the intent is to create what is called "conversational privacy." You can hear the sounds of other people talking in normal voices but their speech is unintelligible.

If you have partitions that do not have much acoustical material applied to them, you might try applying some of your own. Cork tack board, for example, is an excellent sound absorber and also provides you with usable space on partitions. Small woven pieces can also be attached to partitions in the same manner you might attach photographs or paintings, and they serve a double purpose. They personalize your space while also acting as a sound dampener. Another double-edged solution to the problem of walls is to use filing cabinets, shelving, and other storage units as barriers. These come in a variety of sizes, colors, and materials; can generally be easily moved; and, depending upon what you store in them, may act as excellent sound absorbers. They can also serve as a visual screen that psychologically creates boundaries between two different areas without giving the impression of a prison-like fortresss. A friend of mine made a beautiful screen simply by making paper cutouts and hanging them like a curtain. The design opportunities are unlimited and scissors are easily accessible.

Banners and curtains made of different kinds of material have the same kinds of unlimited opportunities. They have the advantage of being highly portable, relatively inexpensive, and easy to make without special skills. Depending upon the weight of the material you use, these kinds of screens may provide some acoustic dampening, but their primary value is in giving a sense of visual separation between areas. Plants are an additional tool for this kind of separation. In many cases they may be even more acceptable than woven materials and other kinds of hanging objects because there are very few people who do not like plants, unlike colors and patterns that might be found in various textile materials. Plants also have the beauty of being a very humane barrier. They have none of the fortress-like image of a line of file cabinets or a partition, and yet they may serve the needs of privacy extremely well when the purpose is simply to remove visual access into an area.

Most people want both visual and auditory privacy. If something has to be sacrificed, visual access more than auditory access is what most people will give up. We find it harder to screen out what others are saying, and are more concerned about others overhearing us, than we are about their seeing us (except in those cases where observing the activity itself reveals damaging or embarrassing information about ourselves). Whether we achieve visual and or acoustic privacy depends in large part upon the tools of privacy we have available. Here's the best way to use what you have available without giving the impression of being anti-social.

Doors

There is probably no clearer statement of the need for privacy than a closed door. Yet in many offices there are strong but informal norms against closing doors. So the placement of the door becomes a clue itself to your accessibility. The door open a crack indicates that you are there, but would rather not be disturbed. The door propped all the way back indicates that you are not only there, but willing to be accessible to others.

One way of coping with office norms that say the door should almost always be open, even when you need concentration privacy, is to keep the door open but to place some kind of a screen within the room that allows others to see in just enough to know whether or not you are occupied or busy. One person's solution to this problem was to place a six-foot-high by four-feet-wide metal shelving unit between his desk and the door, and to place a variety of personal objects and reading material on the shelves. Someone passing by in the hallway could easily look into the office and see that he was occupied without actually coming into the office or knocking. A closed door in the same situation would

Putting a solid cabinet just inside your office effectively screens visual distractions and will deter most casual visitors. Next to keeping a door shut, it's the strongest nonverbal (and nonwritten) privacy statement you can make.

have necessitated breaking into the work or meeting and would be more disruptive than an open door.

In other cases more opaque barriers, such as file cabinets or shelves filled with books, that actually prevent a view into the room may be desirable. They have the advantage of letting others know that you are there (the door is open), but you can be visually screened from potential visitors without communicating a sense of inaccessibility. You can hear their footsteps coming into the office so that you can stop whatever you are doing and put on your "frontstage" face without the visitor knowing that you were sneaking a look at *Shogun* or taking a catnap. If you have a glass door, you can make it opaque by putting any number of things over the glass. If there is an informal norm or official directive about being visually accessible, you might try covering only part of the door, but leaving the open part at the top of the door where someone could see in only if he or she wanted to make a special effort, but which in most cases would effectively maintain your visual privacy without totally cutting off the possibility of visual access.

Office Size

You may not have much choice about the size of your office, but you may be able to vary the level of visual and auditory access into it by how you arrange the furniture. If your desk is positioned directly facing an open door, you greatly reduce the level of visual privacy. Instead, place the desk in a corner of the room where it cannot be seen from the doorway. You can also orient your desk so that you face away from the door. Or, if sitting with your back to the door makes you uncomfortable, orient your desk perpendicularly to the door. The goal is to restrict your eye contact with persons passing by the entrance to your office. Reducing the amount of eye contact will make others less likely to strike up a conversation with you or enter your office than if they can easily maintain eye contact.

Eye contact is critical to social contact. It is one of the reasons we are almost always annoyed by people who wear dark glasses indoors. We cannot really tell whether these people are paying attention to us or not. Eye contact communicates not only that we are accessible, but through our eyes we also say a great deal about how we are responding to what is being said. This is one reason good light is so critical in interview situations. Without it, you cannot easily tell how you are being received, or to know how the other person is feeling so that you can respond appropriately. Reducing the opportunities for eye contact through furniture arrangements that point your face away from major circulation routes, entrances, and windows should contribute to your concentration privacy.

Windows

Who does not want a window on the world? Even in the office, we want to see outside, check the weather, take a break in routine, and avoid a sense of being couped up and claustrophobic. But if you work in an office with windows through which others can see you as they pass by, you may not feel so lucky. Here's how to solve that problem. Through the use of paper, plants, and fabrics, you can create translucent screens that will allow in light but make it difficult—if not impossible—for someone to see with any clarity into your office. Just as partitions can create what I have called communication privacy, various kinds of screens can create visual privacy to aid work concentration. Screens allow others to tell whether you are or are not there without letting them know exactly what you are doing or with whom you are meeting. If this is the level of visual privacy you need, then screens on windows may be an excellent way of allowing in light without sacrificing total privacy.

Location

I have previously mentioned location with respect to the arrangement of your furniture within your own office. To the extent that you have any opportunity to choose the location of your office, think about the different kinds of privacy you need. My own office is located in a relatively inaccessible wing of a large building. People are constantly getting lost trying to find my office. I love it. This means that anyone who does find me really is looking for me, and it means that I get very little "off the street" traffic. For my own workstyle this makes for a good fit. You should select the location of your office so that it compensates for your weaknesses rather than contributing to them.

Ear Screens

In California's Silicon Valley, where there are never enough qualified professionals to go around, employees are encouraged to work any way they work best. Many like music, but tastes range from Mozart to the Grateful Dead. But that is not a problem. Earplugs have come a long way since we bought the hard rubber pink ones for swimming. They are much more comfortable now, and designed to mask the bulk of noise (unwanted sound)

If you can work well with music, electronic sound screens in the form of personal stereo systems may guard against distraction from nearby conversation. Plugged into your ear, these machines give you a high degree of control over what you listen to and do not irritate neighbors with different tastes.

without cutting off access to what you want to hear. Much more desirable for many are self-contained battery-operated stereo headphones like the Sony Walkmen. You hear what you want, and your colleagues what they want. No one has to suffer the indignities of Musak.

White noise is often piped in through the heating ducts to mask the sounds of normal conversations, typing, footsteps, and files banging. It can be individually created and controlled by buying an inexpensive device designed for this purpose (one of them makes the sound of the ocean) which you can "tune" to meet your own requirements. If you are worried about others' reactions, try talking with your colleagues and working out some acceptable alternatives.

Scheduling

Time is another resource that is often overlooked. Is it possible to attain more privacy, and avoid conflict, by scheduling your activities differently? Cats establish "time territories" in which different cats traverse the same paths, but at different times, so that they avoid running into each other. College students living in dormitories do the same thing: they use a single room at different times of the day or night.

The beauty of this approach is that it may not even need any elaborate discussions. You simply observe closely when those who are being distracting are not around, or when they are more distracting. You then can try to pattern your own schedule in counterpoint to theirs. If they are quieter in the morning, building to a crescendo by late afternoon, why not schedule as many of your meetings as possible during the afternoon, when their voices are not as disruptive to your concentration, and may even serve as a useful form of white noise. You can do your concentrated work in the mornings. You might also come in earlier, or leave later.

Another side of scheduling is the possibility for creating activity zones, or special-use areas. These might be a special area—a quiet zone—carved out of a large group of offices, or it might involve you and a friend whose office has some different characteristics from yours (yours is large and noisy, perfect when room is needed, but terrible for concentration; his, small but quiet) working out a schedule so that you both end up in the office suited to what you are trying to do at the moment. Activity or special zones can be used at certain times of the day, be available on a first-come, first-served basis, or have a sign-up sheet. Start by asking yourself, "What do I really need? What am I willing to give up that someone else might want?" Go bartering.

Lights

If you are reluctant to close your door, one way to achieve concentration privacy is to light up your desk or reading area with a desk lamp, and dim the overhead light. The appearance you give is that you are terribly involved with something and cannot be disturbed.

Shared Rooms

The form of scheduling most evident in most offices today is the shared conference room. These rooms are especially evident in open office designs. Individual employees typically have insufficient room to meet with three or four others, and not enough acoustical privacy to prevent their discussion from being overheard by others. One solution is to dot the landscape with small conference rooms. In theory, they make sense. In practice, they work less well. They often become the large private space of the one or two individual offices next to them. Squatter's rights prevail. They also make spontaneous meetings difficult, since meetings have to be scheduled. Getting up and moving to a conference room, finding out whether one is available (and if it is occupied, looking for another), starting the meeting because the room is empty and then being evicted by scheduled users interrupts the sense of involvement and train of thought critical to quality thinking and discussions.

Since all events in the office are grists for the rumor mill, taking a colleague to the conference room for a meeting may also be misinterpreted by the ever watchful eyes of other employees. The intended popping in and out of conference rooms on an "as needed" basis may become dreaded treks for traumatic events such as performance evaluations. As a result, such reviews may become perfunctory or not take place at all. They become emotionally charged, dreaded experiences because, paradoxically, privacy becomes very public.

Coming into work early, or staying late, when the office is very quiet, may also be good times to schedule meetings. Lounges and cafeterias at low tide may be appropriate since they offer the cover of getting a bit to eat or a cup of coffee. The point of scheduling is simple: Fit your activities into the natural ebb and flow of office events.

Signaling: Body Privacy and Other Hints

You may have well-intentioned colleagues who seem to visit just when you do not want to see anyone. Maybe you need to give them clearer signals about when you are or are not available. Secretaries serve this screening function, but personal secretaries are becoming rarer, and counting on getting one in the future is about as good a bet as a thirty-cent gallon of gas. Doors are also a handy communication device, but many new offices have dispensed with them. What can you do to communicate your accessibility without screaming, "Leave me alone!"?

You need to devise some signaling systems. These might be formal ones, adopted by a whole group after some discussion, in which the presence of a figurine (with its hands over its ears, eyes closed, and lips sealed?) on the corner of your desk is agreed to mean, "Please don't bother me now. I'll be glad to see you later." They system might even be more refined, with different codes expressing different degrees of accessibility: Red means "Please don't bother me under any circumstances," while green means "You can interrupt me if it's critical." Unless you give some clues to your neighbors that you do not want to be bothered, how are they going to know whether or not you want to be left alone?

You might also try body position. Patrons at bars have known for a long time that you leave a person huddled over a drink alone, even if that person is in the middle of a noisy bar. What is your orientation to your office entrance? If you sit facing the entrance, with people passing by in corridors outside, it is tough to concentrate. The impulse is to glance up every time someone passes by. The message, willingly or not, when you make eye contact with some of these passers-by is that you are accessible. At the very least social graces may make it difficult to avoid at least a perfunctory "Hi, ya, Sam." That can easily be dozens of interruptions an hour, each one taking a little time to recover from.

Why not reorient your desk so that you sit perpendicular to the entrance, rather than facing it? You avoid the uncomfortable feeling of being sneaked up on from behind and yet by a subtle twist of your shoulders you can avoid the tendency to look up every time someone passes by. At the same time, you communicate by your "huddle" position that you are hard at work. When you want to be more accessible, you can simply angle your shoulders toward the entrance, thereby making eye contact easier and communicating accessibility.

Copywriter Sandy Gurowitz likes to sit with her back facing the door. She says, "I can sense or hear when somebody comes to the door, but I don't have to stop what I'm doing in quite the same way I would if I were facing the door and I would immediately look up if someone appeared there." With her desk facing away from the door, "When I'm writing and someone comes to the door I finish my thought and then I turn around and say, or maybe even not turn around and say, "What can I do for you?"

Since many people are concerned about appearing antisocial, even though this may be exactly what they need to be for a period of time, strategies that communicate accessibility without appearing aggressively antisocial are important. I have talked about many of them already. They generally fall into placement of furniture and screens that allow others to look into your office without your noticing them, or their necessarily being able to see who is in with you or what you are actually doing. Curtains and opaque glass that transmit light but indicate only shadows or vague movement are an example of the latter, and file cabinets and bookshelves placed near the entrance are common examples of the former.

PRIVACY: WHEN TO AVOID IT

Privacy is important, but how it is used varies across professions. Accountants and attorneys deal with sensitive, personal information that may be embarrassing to the client, and that at the very least is highly confidential. Stockbrokers and journalists, on the other hand, are plugged into constantly changing information networks. (The equivalent of six 100-page novels comes across newspaper wire services every 24 hours.) Interaction and the sharing of information are probably more critical to their effectiveness than the ability to concentrate.

Having easy visual and verbal access to each other makes sharing information and communicating a sense of excitement easy. "To me, being in a large newsroom surrounded by all the confusion and the other reporters gives me a sense of what I'm doing. It generates a certain amount of excitement and purpose," says news reporter Don Ross.

The old-fashioned bullpen also speeds along what sociologists call "work socialization": learning the tricks of the trade. Stockbroker Cornish notes that "It also helps to have the new people listen to the experienced ones selling or describing products."

Newsrooms have similar qualities. At the *Ithaca Journal*, a member of the Gannett newspaper chain, desks are arranged in small clusters of four. Surfaces are piled high with papers, notes, and books. In the morning before deadline the place hums. People pound out the last lines of their day's stories on electric typewriters and electronic word processors while editors look on making comments, suggestions, and revisions. People dart back and forth consulting with each other, and shooting brief questions to those around them. Help with everything from spelling to the person to call for a quick check of a news item happens without stopping the flow of work.

In the afternoon, after deadline, the place thins out and quiets down. The sharing of information, leads, contacts, and ways of structuring a story continues. For the green reporter, like a neophyte stockbroker, the access to experienced hands is invaluable on-the-job training. It is vital to learning the trade. Private offices, and even low partitions separating work stations and making casual visual surveillance difficult, would slow down, if not eradicate, the learning process and completely transform the active, social, group orientation of the entire newsroom staff.

THE BEST APPROACH TO PRIVACY

Which type of privacy do you want, and what tools for getting it will work best for you? It depends on your particular situation and the resources available. Experiment. Explore with your colleagues some different things you might try that are both affordable and acceptable. Do it in a spirit of inquiry. If the first thing you try does not work, do not give up. Find a fabric you and your working neighbor both love; move your desk around again; reschedule activities that require concentration privacy for first thing in the morning.

CHAPTER FOUR

Power

We usually lump status and power together, and assume that more status means more power. But power and status are not the same. Status is your position or rank in relation to others. It defines your relative prestige, which may or may not be a function of your real power. Power is your ability to influence others' behavior. No matter where you sit in the official office hierarchy, your office can gain you more power because it influences your own and others' behavior. Even the smallest design elements can communicate power and influence. The right table shape and seating patterns can affect your leadership or your participation in groups, and the quality of your office environment can have a strong impact on how others assess you, including their impressions of your competence, credibility, and openness.

HOME TURF ADVANTAGE

Power is determined by your physical surroundings, but it is also a function of who lays claim to the area. Meeting with people on your home turf makes a difference. You feel stronger, able to fight harder, and more willing to defend yourself. We do not give up all these characteristics when we cross some magical boundary from our turf to the next person's, but we tend to be less effective. A major advantage of home turf is that it gives you the ability to control what goes on in it. Generally, the more business you can conduct in your own office, at your own desk, the more effective you will be.

As one advertising executive noted, "When I am in the client's office, my ideas are not accepted with as much enthusiasm or as readily as they are here." The difference is the level of control the home turf provides: "When I am in a meeting with a client here, there are no interruptions. When I am at the client's place of business there are so many interruptions and they haven't figured out yet how to provide that safe environment. Those interruptions interfere with productivity. I also think they interfere with my credibility because I try to be a nice guy about it instead of being a bastard. Instead of saying to them, hey, why don't you tell your employee not to keep coming back asking if you have a 8 AA in a shoe. I eat humble pie and I think the relationship suffers."

The greater your ability to structure the pattern of interaction, the greater your influence is likely to be. In some cases your goal may be to relax the person to "soften him up." In other cases it is to structure the interaction so that your own credibility is enhanced, by sitting at the head of a table rather than at the side, for example. It often means gaining the other person's full attention. I first learned of this from a perceptive film maker who arranged to show important videotapes to his state legislators, but the legislators were not paying attention. The problem was that videotapes can be played in a lightened room. As a result, people came in and out, the phone rang, and attention was constantly diverted from the impact of the film. Once he started using 16-mm film, which had to be shown in a specially darkened room, the legislators had to move to a room beyond the reach of their phones. It made for a well-received presentation. What you can learn from that is, first, the importance of using space to get attention, but also the value of lighting down for important personal interaction. Lighting up your seating or meeting area and dimming other lights without darkening the room makes one's attention span more focused.

THE POWER OF ICEBREAKERS

First meetings are often awkward, but they do not need to be so. While it is true that as we get to know people the environment becomes less important as a factor influencing our impressions of them, it is also the case that if the first impressions are sufficiently negative we may never take the extra steps necessary to get to know them better. The more comfortable people are with you, the more likely they are to really hear what you have to say and to respond positively to it. Your office decoration can be a tremendously effective tool for putting others at their ease.

Insurance agents, advertising executives, accountants, and lawyers often use their surroundings to get first meetings off to a good start. If they do not get past this point, they do not get anywhere. It is definitely a power position. Personal artifacts and memorabilia are excellent icebreakers. People want to feel comfortable with the person from whom they are buying a product or service. And the best of way of doing this is by getting to know that person.

In one conference room into which I was ushered to meet with the head of an advertising firm, the walls were covered with photographs, drawings, and excerpts of speeches of Abraham Lincoln. Lincoln's bust adorned the conference table. In other offices the walls were draped with pictures of family and personal photos and autographed baseballs rested on the credenzas. These kinds of environmental artifacts are meaningful for their office-owners, but their usefulness extends to breaking the ice with new clients. As ad executive J. B. Graves says, "I like to deal with people's comfort. I try to make them very comfortable. In any environment icebreakers can help give them something to talk about. Every time people walk in this room they talk about Abraham Lincoln. He was honest, he was legendary, he did a lot of things. There are all kinds of little facets to his existence. It helps. It warms things up. People start talking about him. You never know what angle they are going to hit on, but they are going to talk about him."

The use of personal memorabilia is especially evident in small offices. Insurance agent Dave Banfield has photographs of geese in flight and watercolors of birds sharing the wall with photographs of family members. Autographed baseballs and papier-mâché pencil holders sit on tabletops. Banfield does not claim that the environment affects his ability to sell per se, but that it is a door opener. "It gives people something to comment about when they come into a particular office. All of us have things in our offices that are unique. One partner has an old fireman's hat, another one has an couple of old watercolors that are unique, and people will come in, look around—Oh, are those your kids, did you take these photos—You have spent thirty to forty-five seconds breaking the ice and you get into what they are there for." Other more systematic studies by psychologists support this intuitive grasp of the environment's potential. Studies have found that sculpture and other objects placed in waiting rooms can help break the ice and make people feel more comfortable.

DESIGNING YOUR OFFICE FOR POSITIVE FEEDBACK

Home turf is your prime preserve for getting and giving feedback. Letting others know how they are doing and finding out where you yourself stand are critical to your personal satisfaction, effectiveness, and image of power. The old adage has it that if someone fights with you, at least you know that person cares. Indifference is the stuff of depression, aimlessness, and, therefore, powerlessness. We want people to respond to us, preferably with shouts of "Great job" and "That's the way to go." Loud applause, an elegant lunch on the boss, a raise, or a promotion warm the heart. Yet despite its importance, feedback occurs too rarely in many situations. This is doubly true of negative feedback.

How can your office design affect the amount of feedback and interaction you are able to give—and get? It does this by simulating your availability to others within your company. If your office can accommodate it, place two chairs away from your desk, facing a corner or surrounding a small cafe-type table. You will give the appearance of having an office-within-an-office, a more private place to meet with others for an exchange of ideas. The look will be egalitarian, but since it is your home turf, you are in charge.

Your office's influence stems from its ability to make certain kinds of interactions and certain kinds of behavior harder rather than easier. Just as water seeks its own level, we tend to flow in the direction of least resistance. Before you conclude that your office is important primarily for how it makes you feel, look at how it structures your interaction with colleagues, clients, and employees. Side-by-side offices do not guarantee interaction of any kind, let alone productive interaction. But if you are inclined to interact with your neighbor, this arrangement can significantly facilitate it. Knowledge workers need contact with others to share information, try out ideas, and exchange tips and gossip. Any way in which your office can facilitate these kinds of interaction becomes critical. It is difficult to influence anyone if you do not have access to him or her. You can write a memo, buzz people on the intercom or call them up on the computer, but the most effective forms of social influence are still based on face-to-face contact.

THE OFFICE AS A MIRROR IMAGE

In power situations, your office is like a second skin. It conveys your image, for better or worse, by reflecting your values, your capabilities, your personality—all the factors upon which decisions about you are made.

Probably because they are trained to create them, advertising people are particularly sensitive to the impact that the office image can have on clients, because it may be the deciding factor between winning and losing an account. While we often think of stereotypes negatively, one ad executive observed that a successful image depends on the effective use of stereotypes. "You want people to put you in the right categories. You want them to do it immediately. The idea is to get them to push the right button: Schmuck or Ace. Does this person have his act together or is he working out of a suitcase?" Impression management is a form of social influence—or power—that all of us are concerned about. But we fail to use it effectively when we confuse who we really are with who we think we should be in someone else's eyes. You will make the best impression when you are comfortable. Do not buy high tech when you really like

Early American. Extremes in taste are always dangerous unless you are very secure or in a creative business where eccentricity is appreciated.

One way of becoming sensitive to the image you want to convey is to pay attention to how you respond to others' image-making. I always thought that I appreciated "homey" in almost any situation until my first visit to a family doctor when I arrived in Ithaca. To my own surprise this doctor's office completely undermined my confidence in his capabilities. The office was located in a small shopping center. The inside of the waiting room was more like the living room of a student co-op than my image of a doctor's office. The furniture was beat up, the bookcase had one or two tumbled-down books, and the rugs were threadbare. A sense of professionalism was totally absent. I wanted a friendly and informal relationship with the doctor, but I also wanted someone who was "keeping up." "Homey" in an office setting requires a balance of things comfortable and coolly professional.

In many professions, the problem is not simply showing that you are "keeping up" but doing this in a way that avoids any association of "modern" with "institutional." We want an office to look clean and modern, but we also want it to be friendly, inviting, and reassuring. How you communicate modernity varies, but a common component today centers around electronics and computers. John Dieters-Hagen, a partner in a small accounting firm, finds that the new computer the firm purchased for its office saves it money. But another asset is helping project a "leading-edge" image. This firm can lay claim to being the first in a small city to have its own computer facilities, and that becomes part of its marketing strategy as much as the personal characteristics, qualifications, and experience of its employees.

For others, the clean, modern business image is obtained without sacrificing an image of friendliness by using traditional materials like polka-dotted fabrics, butcherblock furniture, and other modern versions of traditional designs. The designs avoid the high-tech look of chrome and glass. The fabrics are warm-toned without being bright and harsh. I have seen these kinds of furnishings used to create a warm and friendly, but still businesslike, atmosphere in accountants', architects', and publishers' offices.

Image is crucial for maintaining power, but it does not have to be big-city slick. Michael Korda once defined a simple black one-line, no-hold-button telephone as a power tool par excellence, because while it was not modern or glamorous, it conveyed a secret "hot-line" impression. You do not have to go to such lengths, however, to "dress down" for power. To be slick without looking slick, the trick is to be different. Clients will often appreciate the opportunity to get away from their own offices to one that is different. In one small advertising agency the offices were deliberately created to contrast with many of its clients' own offices. The company's president wanted to make his office a place where his clients wanted to come to. "I don't think a place like this should be boring at all. I think it should be very exciting. I think clients want that. They're in boring environments themselves and they like to come down; they really enjoy being here. And I can do a hell of a lot of business with them when they want to come here. Our coke machine has beer in it, and my account executives or I don't have to leave this building. People like to come here just because of the environment. And they've got beautiful offices, most of them. The people we represent have already made a lot of money and they've gone beautiful places, but they like to come here and it's not because it's a great big expensive office complex. In fact, it was done on the most modest budget you can image."

From the Rolling Stones played over the office PA system to Abraham Lincoln memorabilia hanging on the black walls of the conference room to the wicker chair hanging from the ceiling in one of the copywriters' offices it is easy to see why visitors would like this ad agency. It is deliberate without being forced. None of the materials is expensive, but some of them, like the black paint in the conference room, are unusual. What seems like a harsh, if not bizarre, color selection is tremendously softened by the traditional and soft images provided by the Lincoln memorabilia, much of it in old wooden frames.

We are more likely to accept the idea that the offices of an advertising agency can convey an unconventional image because they are selling creativity, which most people believe comes in a nonstandardized package (at least for others!). In a business like insurance the problem may be more complex because both the nature of the product and the service's professional status are more ambiguous. Many insurance agents think of themselves as professionals, and want their clients to think of them in the way they think about attorneys and account-

ants. Cients' perceptions range from door-to-door salesman and hard-selling huckster to quasi-professional. So
some firms, in an effort to communicate a professional
image, enlist their office environment in their cause.

Bill Scott, owner of a small insurance agency in upstate New York, recently moved his firm into a lavishly
renovated office on a major downtown street. The office
is very businesslike, modern, and efficient. Its modern
oak furniture, exposed brick walls, and gray cut-pile
carpeting proclaim in no uncertain terms, "We're professionals here." The expensive but not traditional materials and quality detailing effectively communicate a very
successful businesslike image without seeming hard and
impersonal.

Office images are created to influence behavior, to win
clients—to gain power. People tell Scott how much he
had done for Downtown by doing a quality renovation,
and he readily admits that he loves the constant backpat-
ting and effusive compliments. He should. It works for
him. Everytime Scott looks around and sees his oak
desk, carpeting, and brick wall he has visible evidence of
his own success. His office tells him that he is a professional eight hours a day. Since the majority of his clients
are commercial firms rather than individuals, it is appropriate. If all his clients were individuals looking for car
and homeowner policies, it might be overwhelming.

To know whether the image works for your clients,
you need to know what kinds of clients you have now,
and what kind you want to attract. How do the clients
see themselves? What do they think insurance people
like? Which button are you pushing? I cannot help but

think of the millionaire used-car salesman who drove a beat-up Chevy that he parked in front of his shack on the used-car lot. He knew that used-car buyers would be suspicious of the kind of deals they were getting from a used-car salesman rich enough to drive a Cadillac and own an elaborate showroom.

WHEN IS A "BEAUTIFUL" OFFICE A "POWER" OFFICE?

Most of us spend an inordinate amount of time talking to others. Hiring decisions, promotions, performance evaluations, and judgments of personal capabilities and limitations, motivations, intentions, and so on are part of both the formal and informal activities of most of our jobs. The idea that your office environment can influence these kinds of judgments and decisions seems outlandish to most people. But a number of studies suggest that the environmental conditions under which such decisions are made can influence such things as salary adjustments and one's liking and perception of one's colleagues.

Two early studies, done over twenty-five years ago, looked at the effects of "beautiful," "average," and "ugly" rooms on the perception of "energy" and "well-being" in faces. Up until this time most studies of environmental effects have been done by human-factors specialists who measured the effects of such environmental characteristics as color, noise, or vibrations on very specific and narrow tasks like memory and motor performance.

Maslow and Mintz decided to look at more social-psychological effects. The "beautiful" room was large and was furnished with attractive and comfortable furniture including a soft armchair and mahogany desk. It had a small table, wooden bookcase, Navajo rug, and drapes and paintings. There were also some sculpture and art objects on the desk and tables. The "ugly" room was described by those who saw it as "horrible," "disgusting," and "repulsive." Essentially it was a janitor's closet painted with battleship gray walls, its overhead bulb with a dirty, torn, ill-fitting lamp shade; it was in disheveled condition. Tin cans served as ash trays and windows were adorned with dirty and torn shades. Pails, brooms, mops, and cardboard boxes were strewn around the room. Extremes of environmental conditions to be sure, but at the time it was an innovative idea to even think that the environment might influence social judgment. Did it have an effect?

The people who rated the faces in the ugly room were significantly more negative in their judgments of the faces. They thought the people had significantly less energy and were more "irritable" than "content." Because they were concerned that these effects might only be short-term, they redid the study checking for long-term effects. They found the same results.

The most interesting part of the study was that the people who ran the experiment, and who had to spend time in both the ugly room and the beautiful room, also changed their behavior, although they were totally unaware of this fact. The researchers noted that the examiners in the "ugly" room had such reactions as monotony, fatigue, headache, sleepiness, discontent, irritability, hostility, and avoidance of the room. These same examiners in the "beautiful" room had feelings of comfort, pleasure, enjoyment, importance, energy, and a desire to continue their activity.

The studies leave a number of questions unanswered, but they suggest some fascinating ways your office environment can influence your behavior. More recent studies have looked at less extreme environments with equally unexpected results. One study found that the conventional wisdom that people are more irritable "when hot and grouchy" was supported by laboratory studies. People who participated in the study under conditions of high temperature were much less attracted to their partners in this study than when they participated under normal temperatures. The implications for national policies reducing energy consumption, which raise the effective temperature in office buildings, are worth contemplating here.

There are many simple things you can do to improve the impressions your office makes on others. Psychologists have found that where you place your desk and how tidy you keep your office will affect visitors' comfort and sense of being welcomed. Such small variations in your office design will also affect how competitive, organized, friendly, and confident dealing with visitors others perceive you, as well as their perception of how busy they think you are.

Tidiness can be critical in others' impressions of you, but being absolutely organized is not necessarily any better than being completely disorganized. Researchers at Iowa State University have found that a middle ground, which they describe as "organized stacks," is better than either extreme. People know that you are active and involved, but also see you as in control. An open desk placement, in which your desk does not present a barrier between yourself and your visitors, will make your visitors feel more comfortable and welcome than a closed arrangement, where you desk stands guard between you and whoever comes into your office. An open desk placement also creates the impression of being friendly and confident dealing with others. Status symbols such as degrees and credentials have less impact than tidiness or desk placement, but with these in your office you create the impression of being a higher achiever and having more rank than you would without them.

Consciousness of your environment pays off not only in psychological ways; it can make thousand of dollars of difference. Psychologists at the University of Georgia recently studied the effect of different levels of office noise on salary recommendations. Their theory suggests that our evaluations of people and things are influenced by the positive or negative conditions under which the evaluations are made. A job applicant whose interview occurs over an enjoyable meal, which is a reinforcing condition, is likely to be more positively evaluated than the same person whose interview takes place in a crowed diner on a hot summer day. In experiments, students who played the role of personnel manager and who were asked to assign salaries to persons just hired tended to assign salaries that were on the average $900 less when the students made the recommendations under noisy as opposed to quiet conditions. The "noisy" conditions actually represented a normal office environment. They were created by playing a tape of the sounds from an office in a large insurance company. Sounds included typing, telephones ringing, talking, paper rustling, and people walking and moving. The tape was played at the same sound level that it had been recorded in the actual office. In the "quiet" room, the tape was not played at all.

The implications for your office design should be obvious. At the very least, these findings suggest that whether you make evaluations of others or are being evaluated yourself you might want to influence where these judgements take place. Finding a quiet place to make evaluative decisions, or doing this sort of work at times when your office is relatively quiet, should enhance the quality of your decisions. An ex-parole officer I know observed that the kinds of judgments made about individual offenders and the disposition of cases changed markedly when the parole officers moved from a small storefront office to a more formal facility designed with open offices. The noise and movement of people in and around the office, the constant ringing of telephones, and the tension and energy needed to screen out the distraction of others when interviewing clients or writing reports took their toll. They undermined her sense of power and effectiveness. She felt that decisions were made much more rapidly and without careful consideration of all the implications. The task became one of "getting done." Parole officers were more likely to go home to work, missing some spontaneous contact with clients who came in off the streets, and once at home they tended to get involved in other things besides work.

SEX AND THE POWER-DESIGNED OFFICE

You want others to see you as credible, effective, and authoritative. Our own research suggests that your own sex, as well as the sex of the persons with whom you are meeting, affects which seating position you should choose to enhance these impressions. Be clear about what kind of impressions you want to create and then use the environment to subtly help strengthen—or weaken—them. The effects are likely to be particularly strong on first impressions.

You may also find that your best intentions are making you less effective! Let me explain. My own office has both a large desk and a small round conference table. For years I deliberately moved from my desk to the round conference table whenever students or other visitors came in, without regard to their sex. I was sure that everyone preferred the more informal round table. When I finally asked students where they preferred to sit, and why, I found, to my surprise, that several women preferred sitting facing me across the desk. They wanted a more formal arrangement—the one I had been conscientiously avoiding.

Apparently many of the female students were less comfortable and less relaxed at the more informal round

All of these arrangements are "friendly." The corner-to-corner arrangement is best for comfortable conversation, and separate chairs are better than the sofa because they provide a greater sense of personal space and more psychological security. For male-female interactions especially, these subtle spacial boundaries can increase comfort and reduce anxiety.

Women who want to convey a sense of power and authority should sit at the conference table or—even better—behind a desk. You are thus at equal height; and the comfortable but firm chair makes it easy to maintain an upright position and eye contact.

Sitting at close range, by contrast, can cause subtle feelings of discomfort.

table than they were in the more formal arrangement with me sitting behind the desk. Why? At a round conference table, boundaries are always less clear. At least part of their attention was focused on sexual concerns rather than on the discussion of the paper. What is more, they also thought the more informal arrangement made them less likely to strenuously defend the ideas they came to discuss with me. They felt deprived of power. All of this surprised me, and so I decided to do a more thorough study.

It turned out that male and female students' ratings of either a male or female professor were different depending on where they sat, but not in the way we had expected. Males rated female professors higher on credibility and effectiveness at the round table, and rated men higher on these dimensions at the desk. Women's ratings were just the reverse. Men were seen as more credible and effective at the round table, and women more credible and effective at the desk. It seems that both sexes feel more comfortable when they see persons of the same sex in power positions. Why?

In terms of office design, our study suggests that to appear credible and effective you should try to sit in non-power positions when meeting with persons who may be threatened by your power or authority, exactly the case for many mixed-sex meetings. Furniture arrangements that provide clear boundaries, such as a square conference table in which each person has a side, may help create a more positive impression with visitors of either sex than sitting at a round table or at a couch. If your goal is to maximize the impression of friendliness and openness, a less formal arrangement such as at a small conference table is a good bet whether meeting with a man or woman.

You can explore some of the effects of furniture arrangement on your own behavior and on others' response to you by doing simple mini–experiments. Rearrange the furniture to create more or less of a barrier between yourself and your visitors. What differences do you notice in their behavior or your own? Are you more open in some situations than in others? Are you more likely to challenge? Is the challenge more or less aggressive? Do you get the feeling that your visitors, clients, or colleagues are more or less likely to challenge you under some situations? Not only will you probably have a more efficient office, but you may also gain some valuable new insights into your own behavior.

DO YOU WANT TO SIT AT THE TOP? IT IS ALL WHERE YOU SIT ON THE WAY UP

When we think of power as the ability to influence people, we often think of leaders as prime examples of power-wielders. Leaders take initiative, guide discussions in particular directions, suggest solutions. Karl Weick, a leading organizational psychologist, notes that contrary to our common conception of a leader influencing all the followers, in fact, it is the followers who confer on the leader his or her influence. For your boss to be a leader, you have to agree to be lead. Leaders can be charismatic personalities; but participation, a critical component of effective leadership, can be influenced by your furniture arrangement as well as by your personality. The best arena for leadership are the conference room or the meeting area in your own office.

A "neutral" conference must be transformed into a positive interaction support system. Where you sit at that rectangular conference table is more than a minor concern. Robert Sommer, a pioneer in the study of how furniture arrangement influences social interaction, found that people who sit at the head of a rectangular table are much more likely to participate verbally in group discussions than those people sitting along the sides of the table. If you sit at the head of the table, you also are more likely to be perceived and selected as a leader than if you sit along the sides of a rectangular table. Sommer found that people arrange themselves around a table differently depending on what they are doing. People in a competitive situation choose to sit directly facing each other on opposite sides of the table, while persons cooperating tend to sit side-by-side. Those interacting without any cooperative or competitive definition of the situation most often choose to sit in a corner-to-corner arrangement. Moreover, if you sit toward the front and in the center of a room you are much more likely to participate than if you sit toward the side and rear.

Just as successful vintners know intimately the most minute topographical features of their fields and the climatic conditions associated with them, those people wanting to take a more active leadership role need to understand the topography of the conference room and how it affects their participation and effectiveness in meetings.

You also need to be able to read and understand the nonverbal as well as the verbal signals that co-workers send, and the right work area helps in this. The next time you arrange a meeting, take into consideration the degree of familiarity among the group members, the likelihood of tension and conflict, and the personalities of the people involved. Do not just go to the nearest conference room, most often equipped with a long rectangular table set in the middle of the room. You know what happens there. The person who calls the meeting sits at the head of the table, and others file in and sit where they can, pretty much as a function of their order of entering the room.

Instead try for arrangements that maximize eye contact and minimize distances separating people because these arrangements are optimal for encouraging social contact. For such purposes a squared circle is better than a long conference table. The arrangement of the table and chairs is unlikely to make or break a meeting. But it can contribute to productivity through its ability to help you structure the kinds of social relationships that are necessary to develop team effectiveness. The presence of a small conference table in your office contributes to the image of you as a leader: a person who calls meetings and expects to guide discussions rather than always following the lead of others.

Not every group meeting must be held in a conference room; your own office can be a meeting room. The kind of furniture you have there can set up the power plays in your favor, if you are aware of seating arrangements and levels. You can sit behind your desk, facing the people with whom you are meeting, to convey an authoritative image. Or you can sit side-by-side with your guests, away from your desk. This position conveys an accessible, concerned image. Such an image may give you power in the end, as your input into the discussion will be listened to and respected as coming from one of a cooperative team.

POWER TOOLS

Power is the ability to guide behavior and events in particular directions. Communication—both verbal and nonverbal—is critical to your effectiveness. Changing your office lighting or rearranging your office furniture can increase your power by influencing not only the frequency and quality of the contact you have with others, but also the impressions that these others have of you. Power tools are all around your office. You need only to plug them in.

Seating Position

If you want to enhance your participation in groups, sit as much in the center and as close to the front as you can. In small group meetings, if you want to enhance your participation and power, sit facing the most powerful people in the room and within five feet of them.

Avoid sitting down the sides of a rectangular table unless you can face another powerful person from that position.

If you want to be seen as a leader, get to the meeting early enough to sit at the head of the table or close to it. If you are arranging the meeting and want to facilitate interaction and discussion, arrange the chairs or tables in a circle or square. Try to maximize eye contact among the participants.

If you want to maximize cooperation, a side-by-side arrangement at a table is more appropriate and effective than sitting across from another person.

If you are a male and interact with females frequently, some type of barrier, or at least a clear boundary, in a seating arrangement is desirable, especially at first meeting or when you do not know the other person very well. A square desk is better than a round desk, and sitting behind a desk is better than sitting at a sofa. If you are female, whether you interact mostly with men or with women, you will be seen as more powerful and authoritative if you sit behind the desk rather than at a conference table or conversational seating area. This is particularly important on first contact.

Quality and Cleanliness

Avoid making or having decisions made about you in ugly and unpleasant surroundings. If a news reporter is going to interview you, take that person to the most pleasant place you know. Control your setting. If you are going to evaluate others, realize that doing it in noisy, hot, overcrowded surroundings may make your judgments more negative than they would be in pleasant surroundings.

Cleanliness and a sense of order communicate your being in control. They can be obtained without sterility and institutionalization. Keep working files in neat stacks, and if you have the room, reserve a small conference table or your desk as an uncluttered "free space" where you can meet with visitors. Basically, try zoning your office, even if its small: a place to write, a place to talk, a place for storage. Storage shelves that have doors allow you to quickly obscure from view computer printouts, working files, and your own notes and paraphernalia that can mistakenly convey a sense of being overly busy and out of control.

A sense of order calms and relaxes both you and the people you are interacting with. It also helps convey a positive impression about your interest in the other person. One study of college students' reactions to photographs of a professor's office, which was either piled high with books and papers or neatly organized with clean surfaces, found that students who looked at the cluttered office perceived the professor as being too busy to have real time for them.

To be effective you need to convey the sense that you are paying attention to the people you are interacting with, and that you are concerned about them. This does not mean that you have to create an office that looks like a hospital sterile room. People respond positively to the fact that others are involved with their work and busy. The point is simply to communicate having a sense of control over your environment, as opposed to its control-ling you.

Also remember that while backstage areas may be more informal and less ordered than frontstage areas, they should not undermine the overall image you are trying to convey. If you control a backstage area that is infrequently visited by outsiders, an effective means of dealing with the occasional visitor is to go along with that person and help interpret what may seem like disorder as a high level of productive activity.

Lighting

In any communication process you want to find out as much information as possible about the other person's response to what you are saying, as well as to convey information accurately to that person. Lighting is a critical component in such information exchanges. In dim lighting a great number of facial cues and other nonverbal behavior are lost that provide a real context for helping interpret the verbal content of the communi-cation. Strong light behind your back makes it much harder for someone talking with you to see you clearly. That person loses important nonverbal cues about your own behavior, and what you gain in control of informa-tion about yourself is bought at the expense of the other person's comfort. He or she is straining to see you and often feels uncomfortable and shortchanged about the meeting.

Do not locate your desk with a window behind it if visitors will sit facing you during meetings unless you have curtains that can be pulled when strong light is coming through the window. Good, clear directional light lets you read cues from others' behavior without creating the feeling of being in a short-order restaurant or under the interrogator's bare light bulb. Flexible desk lamps come in dozens of styles and colors and they can be clamped to tabletops, hung on the wall, or laid on a desk or floor. Most of them are quite inexpensive and they can be bought at almost any store that sells home furnishings. To create a soft, warm atmosphere, try bouncing the light off other surfaces. Architects call this "washing the walls" with light.

You can bring in your own desk lamps, and if you have overhead fluorescent lamps see whether it is possible for the maintenance people to replace the cooler colors with daylight fluorescent lamps. If you find yourself talking with someone who is strongly backlighted, ask that person to pull the blinds or change your position slightly so that you are sitting on an angle that shifts the light to one side.

Meeting Location

You will be more effective if you can convey your messages without interruption. Invite others to your office rather than going to their offices. If that does not seem appropriate, or if you cannot control interaction in your own office, suggest a neutral location *with which you are familiar*. Do not meet at a restaurant unless you have been there before and know that you can find a quiet table. If you are at someone else's office and find that you are continually interrupted, politely ask whether the other person would not like to go somewhere where you will not be interrupted. Make it clear that you would like to move so that you can concentrate more effectively on what the other person has to say, rather than suggesting that he or she is not paying attention to you.

Equipment and Paraphernalia

I have mentioned earlier how various kinds of objects in the office can be used to create particular images. You need icebreakers to put people at ease and to give them something to respond to that lets them share information about themselves as well as learn something about you. Since people are different and you cannot know what everyone's interests are, provide a variety of objects. Signed baseballs attract the sports minded, but scenic photographs, family pictures, or achievement certificates and diplomas have a more general appeal.

As you think about power, remember that real leaders have willing followers. Others are more likely willingly to work with rather than against you when they feel they are treated fairly and their views have been heard. Knowing how seemingly insignificant details of furniture arrangement and lighting influence effective communication, you can now work to put yourself in power positions where you are more likely to be seen and heard the way you want to be seen and heard.

PART THREE
Styles of Office

CHAPTER FIVE

The Creative Office

Creativity is not bound to particular professions. In its appropriate form it is as likely to be found in the stockbroker's or attorney's office as in the ad writer's or artist's. Yet professions such as writing, architecture and design, advertising, and fashion have creativity at their core. They are set apart because we expect the people who practice them to be a little eccentric. We are wary of the advertising copywriter who looks like a stockbroker or the lawyer who dresses like an artist.

At the heart of the creative office is personal control of the environment. More so than in other types of offices, the physical surroundings for creative work must respond to constantly changing moods and energy levels. Creativity is not a light switch flicked on and off at will. Intense periods of sustained concentration may be followed by total relaxation. Concentration itself may take different forms, ranging from being glued to a typewriter to pacing before a huge easel to sitting on a couch reflecting over a new idea. The creative office must permit all these things. But if it is inspirational too—if it is beautiful or especially cheery—so much the better.

At creative peaks designers, writers, or architects may appear to a casual observer to be doing nothing. The next instant they may be pounding on the typewriter or totally engrossed in a drawing. Creative activity is a backstage phenomenon. It requires a place where you can devote total energy to the work itself without siphoning it off to project the impression of work or to engage in social niceties. The need to avoid such social responses is why so much creative work is usually done at home or in a separate studio rather than at the "office."

Because creative activity is largely asocial, your workspace, unlike client-centered offices, should therefore be organized with a single purpose in mind: your own comfort. Others' may enter your creative space at times, but they do so on your terms, not theirs. You may want people's response to your work and ideas, but this kind of social activity precedes or follows creative bursts more often than it is an integral part of them. Control over the environment for creative work should include the opportunity for access to people. But social stimulation must be initiated by the person doing the creative work when it is wanted, rather than allowing it to take the form of unwanted interruptions dictated by others' needs. For this reason, concentration privacy is critical to creative work. It is not necessarily synonymous with quiet, but it does provide total control over what particular sounds, sights, and distractions enter into the workspace, and at what times.

The romance of the starving artist working in cold, damp, cramped space is more fiction than fact, and certainly more dictated by necessity than by choice.

After the success of his first play, Moss Hart walked out of his dreary little apartment without looking back. He could not close the door quickly enough on his former life style. Artists from Picasso to Maurice Sendak design their studios with great attention to the qualities of space, light, and arrangement. It is hardly a matter to be treated indifferently. Cramped space may produce cramped and small-minded work. A design educator I know was astonished when a sculpture class he had taught for years in a small room with low ceilings was moved into a new, much larger studio with high ceilings. Just as work expands to fill the time, the sculpture expanded to fit the space. Student work was two and three times as large in the new studio.

A good creative environment energizes and motivates. From objects with personal histories and meanings to one's own work and work tools, creative workspace should stimulate the creative juices. Unlike more social offices, where the impression conveyed to others through the choice of everything from furniture to art objects is made taking into consideration how others might respond, the creative office is highly personal. Both the behavior and objects in it are relatively unfiltered by others' expectations of what is appropriate, desirable, or "right." At the very least, a creative environment should not grate, irritate, or exacerbate. Light should fall where you need it, the tools of your trade (whether word processor or paintbrush) should be available when needed and conveniently stored when not needed; and the space should be accessible to you at any time of the day or night.

Workspace by itself cannot invent creativity, nor can it totally suppress it. But it makes little sense to try and nourish creativity in unpleasant, uncomfortable, and unsuitable workspace. For the dedicated and driven, this is possible, but it is hardly worth the immense amount of energy a quality work environment could save for more productive purposes.

In this chapter we look at several different kinds of offices used by people in creative professions, and how these people have shaped their offices to enhance their own creativity and effectiveness. Visually they are some of the most exciting because, whether in small business or large corporation, there is a greater acceptance of the need for people in professions like design and advertising to create spaces that support and reflect their own very strong individuality.

ZONING CREATIVE SPACE

The name Herman does not ring the kind of bells that Lauren, Halston, or Cardin do, but in the 1960s Stan Herman was on that kind of track; he was one of the hottest ready-to-wear designers in America. Winner of fashion's most prestigious awards—the Coty American Fashion Critics Award and the "Winnie"—Herman has traveled a long distance since designing sexy "table top clothes" for the cocktail hour. For a variety of reasons he decided to step out of the glamorous but ferocious pace of Seventh Avenue to move into the less hectic world of corporate design—uniforms. The next time you are served a hamburger at McDonald's look at the uniform of the person serving you. You will see the stamp of Herman. Beyond this work on corporate uniforms, an elegant line of lingerie helps Herman keep his hand in the more glamorous end of the fashion market. By freelancing Herman can "lead the clean life in a nice studio," since in the larger world of fashion design an attractive workspace can be a rarity.

Unless designers have their own firms, they are more likely to work "under terrible conditions" than in anything resembling luxury space. They are often relegated to windowless back rooms while pleasant frontstage areas are reserved for customers. The reasons for this have to do with the deep-seated fashion mentality. Being shoved into corners is, in part, a holdover from sweatshop days, when it was believed that windows encouraged "star gazing." What is more, windows also contributed to paranoia. Designers were terrified of competitors' spies using binoculars to peer through studio windows and thus learn the coming season's fashion secrets.

Herman's own New York City studio has very high ceilings with huge arched windows overlooking Bryant Park. His primary intent in creating this studio was to make it a comfortable, warm, pleasant space, where he does not feel "hemmed in." This is especially important because Herman does not sit alone waiting for the Muses to visit. He has to work alone on his designs, but he cannot work privately. For him, creative space must accommodate several assistants and a bevy of models. How can he accomplish so many tasks in a single studio

Refinished wooden floors, an oak wardrobe, and a round oak table create the warm, comfortable, soft-edged environment fashion designer Stan Herman wants for his studio.

without feeling crowded? By zoning the area very carefully.

Anyone in a creative occupation knows that a workspace must accommodate several tasks. It must be a place in which to do the physical act of designing, writing, or painting; and it must be a place to think, rest, and gain perspective and inspiration. Even in the smallest office or studio it is best to create two separate work stations for these separate activities. Zoning is the ideal way to do this. By setting up a couch or an easy chair away from your desk, you can withdraw for a needed boost of energy. You might also arrange this extra seating in an area where you and others can meet and brainstorm.

The Creative Office

Herman's office is zoned by furniture arrangements—not walls—into distinctly different types of work area. From the entrance the first thing you see is Herman's own workspace. This is where he draws, meets with clients, works out details with his assistant, and handles other administrative and personal matters. Off this area are other areas where the designs are transformed from lines on paper to actual prototype garments. Three other assistants cut and sew in these areas as well as in the balcony on the second floor.

As a workspace for a closely knit design team, the studio functions beautifully because it separates different functions—design, pattern making, cutting, sewing, draping—from each other. Yet because of the openness of the space, people can yell to each other, ask questions, and get a sense of the overall operation. No one is shoved into a back corner. In a small studio such a "family" feeling can make the difference between getting the work out and missing a deadline. The only drawback, which Herman laughed over as he described it, occurs when clients meeting with him downstairs at the round oak table in a very serene, relaxed atmosphere are jerked upright by the sudden sounds of angry women arguing in the balcony above. Herman is more than willing to risk these occasional outbursts because of the advantages the openness provides.

Like a good museum, this creative space is pleasant but not obtrusive. It allows the designers themselves and their colors and patterns to stand out. The quality of light and color in the main studio room is simple, subtle, and very warm. Most of the light is natural and comes

The round oak table provides a place away from his work desk for Herman to relax, and doubles as a conference table when clients visit. The informality of this meeting area complements Herman's own low-key style.

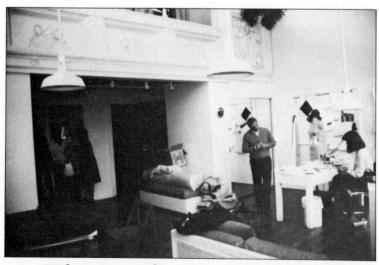

With sewing and cutting rooms upstairs and draping rooms downstairs adjacent to the central work area, the studio becomes a self-contained world. The space is shared and open; trust and courtesy are a must here.

Herman's desk is only a few feet from his assistant's. Communication, therefore, is easy and on-going.

through the large east windows. Incandescent lights hanging from the ceiling throw a soft light. The furnishings are neutral in tone: either a dark oak or white. Colorful fabrics and designs casually strewn around the studio add life and vitality.

Similarly like a museum, the studio is sparsely furnished, and what is there has a residential character. An old round oak table is used as the conference table; it doubles as a place to have tea or to grab lunch. An old oak wardrobe closet adds a sense of warmth and a pleasant well-used quality to the space. And two white Parsons tables, a couch, and Herman's desk in the center of the room, near his assistant's, account for the rest of the items. The closeness of the desks makes communication with his assistant easy. Herman selected his assistant knowing that she would have to be a person with whom he could share any secrets. In the open studio space "I have no privacy. Its a very personal place to work. If there was somebody next to me I didn't trust, I would be hysterical."

The sofa is more than just another place to sit. It is a central element in the design process. Herman's apparel designs are unsurpassed in combining comfort and attractiveness at affordable prices. As a designer Herman wants to know how his clothes will look when they are worn. Having models walking around is not enough. In designing a hospital gown, Herman had his models sit and recline, and even sleep on the sofa in ways that the customer eventually will use the garment.

Herman has succeeded in creating a studio where not only he but the people working for him enjoy coming to work. The lack of tension and good feeling among the people working there owes much to Herman's own personal style, but it is also enhanced by the overall studio environment he has created. His energies are not drawn away from design to dwell on unpleasant surroundings or tension and dissatisfaction among the people he depends on closely to help him produce his work. Herman has found and created a "pure design space." It is designed not for clients but "for me." It reinforces, everyday, who he is and wants to be.

Control over others' behavior is not total, but the people who share Herman's space are much more family than just other employees sharing the same office. More to the point, they are there at Herman's bidding. This is his studio, designed and organized to work for him, and no one is unclear about that. Herman has exercised total control in the shaping of the space itself, from furniture and lighting to the colors and finishes of walls and ceilings. The occasional clients who come to the studio often comment positively about it, according to Herman, but Herman's own comfort and response have dictated the form it has taken, not concern about clients' reactions. This is the kind of control that creates a truly personal and creative workspace.

FITTING CREATIVITY TO BUSINESS

Working in an advertising agency that has over 1,000 employees in New York City alone does not seem a likely home for Creative Group Head and copywriter Phil May, who is more of a country than a city person. But his own office design provides a strong alternative. From his casual clothes to the heavy oak furniture, it is easy to see that May has a definite self-image, one that he has managed to express despite the very different modernistic business image of his firm. May refers to the business types as the "suits." He and many other creative people wear jeans. He has personalized his office to such an extent that it fits him like a second skin—or, more appropriately, a worn pair of jeans.

May's job at Dancer, Fitzgerald, Sample makes him more of a "diplomat than writer," in large part because he is good with people. "You're a judge of other people's work, you schmooz a lot, you're the gray-haired creative guru." His office works well for him in this regard, and it also helps him write when he needs to do so. How he came by the furniture in his present office shows impressive imagination.

To his delight, he found he was entitled to a modest budget of about $2,000 that he could use in any way he liked to purchase furniture for his office. Rather than simply going down to the nearest furniture showroom and picking out a sofa, desk, and a few chairs, May struck a bargain with his boss. May would buy the turn-of-the-century oak furniture he really liked "as if I were buying it for myself." He found pressed-oak chairs with no seats in them and refinished, stained, and caned them. His wife made a seat cushion for the Morris chair, and he refinished the rolltop desk. The "deal" was that if or when May left the firm he would be able to purchase this furniture back from it at the original prices he paid. Thus the personal effort he put into refinishing the furniture was not wasted. He was making an investment. The rolltop desk that he bought at that time for a few hundred dollars is now worth a few thousand dollars. The same kinds of appreciation have occurred with the other oak furniture in the office. It was an innovative way of furnishing his office in a style that suited his own taste and image, and it actually works to the firm's advantage as well. It loses nothing and gains a very satisfied employee.

How does May's office contribute to successful ad campaigns? When he is in the office, May feels that "it belongs to me. I don't know that it helps me create

Bill May's creative, non-distracting office setting.

more, but it doesn't get in the way." Not a stunning office, it releases his creative energies because "there are no sharp edges" to distract or irritate him.

His office helps in specific ways. When an idea or ad line occurs to him, it almost passes by his eyes and then "circles to the back of my head, almost like the news down at Times Square." He tries to capture the line in his head on the typewriter before it vanishes. May has found that for him the best way to do this is to lean back in his desk chair, rest his arms on the arm rests, and pull the typewriter so close that it actually sits "right in my lap." To get it that close he turns the typewriter table around so that he does not have to squeeze his legs in underneath or keep the table at arm's length. His best working position is almost literally "laid back" from the waist up.

He also keeps a radio on and listens to Musak-like music, which he finds a soothing form of white noise. If he puts on music he likes, "I find myself start to listen to a song," which is not what he wants to happen. Even the sofa contributes to his effectiveness. May rarely goes out to lunch. He prefers eating in his office, often by himself, for which he uses the round oak table. He can catch a catnap afterwards and before he resumes work in the afternoon. Rather than slogging through the afternoon he is able to work refreshed and with renewed vigor. For a person whose job can be stressful, as it is when one may be asked at 8:00 A.M. to come up with an advertising campaign, and several specific advertisements, by 3:00 P.M., the opportunity to renew his energy is critical to maintain his enthusiasm and originality.

Not only does his office provide May with the comforts of home in a somewhat alien urban environment, but through the kinds of furniture and objects he has brought in to it he has constant reminders of who he is all around him. The props from various commercials he has worked on contribute to his sense of confidence and accomplishment; they also communicate to the people working for him his own success in the advertising world—without his having to say a word. But as identity cues these items stimulate May's professional confidence, which adds much to the creative capacity of someone who has "to constantly invent from zero an idea you hope is different, entertaining."

May's office also shows that a large corporation can project a very definite image without placing every one of its employees in that same mold. May appreciates that in advertising. "You can be as weird as you want to be as long as you don't come naked or go around flashing." His office is essentially a backstage area designed primarily, but not exclusively, for himself. Most of the "clients" who appear are people working under his direction. When he meets with business clients he goes either to their offices or to the firm's conference and meeting rooms. The personal and the corporate—the "suits" or marketing people and the "jeans" or creative folk—can coexist in this kind of atmosphere. May is not forced to suppress his own work style or personal comfort.

INSPIRED OFFICES

For all creative people—whether author, painter, sculptor, playwright, or choreographer—observations of the smallest details of the everyday world are the true source of inspiration. Seeing something where others see nothing, and then transforming this observation into a form by which others can see differently too, is art.

The workspace itself can never substitute for the inspiration provided willy nilly by the larger world the artist moves through in the course of daily routines. But a successfully creative workspace sustains the artist's connection to his or her immediate surroundings, the wellspring of visual ideas. A "carriage-barn" that was "so sway-backed and had sides bulging out and roof sagging that it looked like it was going to explode in another big snow" has become a place from which Michael Boyd could retreat from the unwanted intrusions of the "real world" without losing his visual connection to the natural landscape that is one of his greatest pleasures, and the source of inspiration for his paintings.

After installing a steel cable that pulled the barn's sides together long enough to figure out what to do next, an architect friend suggested constructing an inside frame to which the rest of the building could be pulled in and attached. The final result is not perfect, but unless you have achieved the financial success of someone like Stan Herman (and not many do), you compromise. "Everybody would like to have a monster studio, just thousands of square feet so you would never run out of space." Form follows income, and on a modest budget Boyd's barn succeeds in making the most of what seemed at first an unsalvagable building.

The large window and skylight transform a workable space into a more inspirational one. Ironically, the architect "was really opposed to having that big window there." Yet to Boyd it is one of the space's redeeming qualities. "I'm always trying to rearrange my drawing table, but I find I really like to sit looking that way, toward the large window, even though the light might be better if I moved my board so my back was to the window. It's not that I really have such a grand view, although it's pretty nice in the summer and fall when the trees are leafed out, but its just nice having that space."

The impact of this landscape on Boyd's work is real but subtle. "If you're really working on something that interests you, it almost doesn't matter where you work. You can work under conditions that would be intolerable if you faced them in a routine job. People working in an office on work that they don't really like doing probably need to give more attention to their surroundings than people who are doing the things they like to do." Does this mean that Boyd could work anywhere or does not care about the quality of his workspace? Hardly.

Like most creative activities, the actual work of producing a product, whether words or visual images or objects, is intense. Much of the time attention has a kind

Michael Boyd is "fanatic" about keeping the studio as clean as possible. Moving around constantly and only rarely sitting, he needs distance to step back and see what he has painted. He wants nothing to divert his eye or energy from his work.

To keep the space open Boyd recently built a compact and efficient rolling workbench, which incorporates material that used to take up more space. Rolled into a corner when painting, he rolls it out into the center of the space when building canvas stretchers or frames.

of laser-beam focus on a particular point or part of the total creative process, oblivious to anything around it. But part of even the most intense work are the brief interludes, the thirty-second pauses in which you pull back and assess what has been done so far. Work has not ceased—far from it—but attention spreads out. It is at these points that the outside world, totally screened from consciousness an instant earlier, pops back into focus. Now Boyd might "notice for the first time that day something about the snow on the roofs or the trees in bloom." The studio windows, a moment before unnoticed, now reestablish the all-important connection to the landscape.

Surroundings are important for Japanese artist Kumi Korf as well. As a child in Japan, Korf remembers her mother reading her a book and, while sitting on her mother's lap, being vaguely aware of the muffled sound of traffic and people's voices floating into the room through the thin shoji screens to create a connection to a larger world while simultaneously keeping it at bay. These and other childhood memories surfaced when Korf moved into her present second-story studio overlooking a pedestrian shopping street.

To screen the bright signs of the stores below she hung some gauzelike material on the windows. "The big step was to put this sheer material on the window opening. I needed to have a kind of relation to the street but I didn't really want to look into and see the stores." Sounds of children playing and crying and adults talking and fighting have the same kind of muffled presence she remembers from her earliest childhood days. The func-

The two windows in artist Kumi Korf's studio appear initially uninspiring. Korf placed sheer material over them to block the view into stores and signs on the city street below. She became fascinated, however, by the play of light and shadow the material created, and the patterns thus formed became the object of her work for several years.

tional response to the unpleasant sight of store signs has become a major inspiration for her paintings.

Although Korf wanted the stores screened, she wanted the light to come in. Once the curtain was in place, she began to observe how the light hit the curtains. "It makes a lot of patterns. They are very simple L-shaped or retangular patterns with enough variation to make it very interesting." The effect of light through the window opening became the subject for a series of paintings using loose graphite collected (in part) from

Look at the gray paintings on the wall. What do you see? The gray paintings are done in loose graphite applied with Japanese brushes and were the initial studies in light and dark inspired by the constantly changing quality of light coming into the studio through the screened windows.

architectural students' pencil sharpeners and applied with soft Japanese brushes to create subtle variations of light and dark.

Like Boyd's studio, Korf's is inspirational not because the space "knocks your socks off" but because some of its simplest, even mundane, characteristics help trigger memories and focus attention in ways that the artist then transforms in their own image to help us—and herself— see the world from a slightly different angle.

CHAPTER SIX

The Administrative Office

Most people, regardless of their particular professions, are responsible for doing some administrative work. For some of us, however, 9 to 5 in a paper kingdom means that most of what we do is prepare financial statements, file records, make telephone calls, and search for information. Administrative offices are distinct from other types of offices because they emphasize such functions.

An administrator has specific office needs. Privacy is typically less of an issue than access to information and people. The sharp roller-coaster-like bursts of energy and intensity found in creative offices are rarer here. Hours are often long. Comfort is important, but tends— unnecessarily—to be downplayed. So is any sign of personal imprint. Administrators are office stoics: their creed is that "a good professional can work anywhere." Traditionally, the best administrative office is, therefore, efficient and businesslike. It is this—and more. In the administrative world, efficiency means order, organization and *comfort*. The proper handling of all these elements will make you better at what you do.

Your chief responsibility is to keep track of what is going on around you. Power comes from being able to obtain information quickly and accurately, whether in files somewhere or in the mind of someone at the other end of a telephone line. Information of all sorts is the critical commodity, and a good office is one that aids its occupants in comfortably handling a constant flow of it. Smart administrators realize that status cues are found in information—in the proper equipment and furnishings. Having your own phone, the latest in storage systems, a CRT on your desk (particularly if it is not shared with others), or an enviably organized filing system are status symbols for an administrative person. They are, as well, critical work tools just as much as is a comfortable easy chair in a client-centered office or an unusual desk or wall hanging in a creative office.

To turn reams of paper into order, comfort, and status is no small task. Here is how a few administrators have successfully done the job by asking two important questions: How do I work best? What does my own office culture deem acceptable? Their answers are as follows.

MAKING ROOM AMID PAPER AND MORE PAPER

Suzanne Rafer works in the birthplace of the best-selling book *Preppy:* Workman Publishers. Some of her best-known acquisitions include *Chili Madness, The*

Teddy Bear Catalogue, and *Shrinklits,* the last a *Times* best-seller in which great works of literature are shrunk down to "ridiculous poems and wonderful illustrations."

At Workman, Rafer's own workspace is in one of the few enclosed offices along the periphery of the floor. When the architect came around with a floor plan and asked, "Which office do you want?" she picked this one—the smallest—because she knew that the company was growing rapidly and the bigger offices seemed big enough to be shared in a space crunch. The last thing she wanted to do was share an office.

Having made the biggest decision, Rafer began to think about what this small office offered. It had glass doors that open onto a kitchen area, and it was a little bit further back from the center of things. The glass doors both appealed and did not appeal. Rafer realized that the view they provided, even if not especially esthetic, would make her own office seem larger. At the same time, the glass doors reduced her visual privacy. She did not give curtains more than passing consideration because she felt that they would make the office more claustrophobic. Instead, she deals with her privacy needs in simple but subtle ways. The simplest is closing the sliding glass doors. This effectively shuts out the sound of most conversations, but not any visual distractions. Yet the way she has arranged her office helps her concentrate and work effectively.

Instead of a desk, Rafer set up two butcherblock tables, while low cabinets and bookshelves she was given served storage and display purposes. Her first thought was to put the butcherblock tables back to back to create a long counter on which she could "spread out text and all the manuscripts in neat little piles" and then roll up and down this "assembly line" in her chair. She tried it briefly but found that the tables along one wall were not particularly social. "All of a sudden it looked like a tunnel." This arrangement also did not do much for visitors. "If anybody came in, you had to whip around. It didn't seem cozy." After experimenting with different arrangements, she found that putting bookcases along one wall and arranging the desks perpendicular to each other worked well. "It cut the space in half and it made my desk a meeting area too."

With this arrangement, this office offers three different positions or functions. Rafer can come out from behind the table and sit in the director's chairs in a circle-like arrangement typical when she meets with editors, agents, and authors. She can also sit at the table perpendicular to the glass doors, where her phone is; and she can sit with her back to the glass doors when she is working at the typewriter actually editing a manuscript.

Rafer uses body language to help reduce visual distractions as well as to communicate her availability. The placement of the desks and chairs is part of a well-thought-out interaction strategy. "Sitting on the work-side of the desk cuts you off from the people you're meeting with and sometimes can cut a meeting short." Sitting at the desk, rather than in the director's chairs, gives her access to many props. "You can ruffle paper, pick up a pen, look like you're interviewing. You can come across as a lot less social." In contrast, "When

Editors need space to concentrate, to meet with writers and their agents, and to provide access to phones and reams of manuscript pages. Two tables in an L-shaped arrangement give editor Suzanne Rafer several different kinds of work zones in a single office. Jacket covers, funny photos, and news stories tacked to the wall are superb icebreakers for first-time visitors, reinforce her own editorial success (and thus her authority), and are a source of ideas when editing or working with writers. White walls and spare furnishings help create a sense of spaciousness in a medium-sized office.

you're meeting on the social side of the desk, you're sitting on angles looking three-quarters at somebody. With full face," which is more likely when sitting on the workside of the table, "any little facial expression can be picked up more readily and read. Choosing the side you sit on says a lot."

Which side she chooses depends on how well she knows the people with whom she is meeting. If she knows them well, sitting on the work side does not make much difference. If she is relatively unfamiliar with them, it can make a difference, and then she chooses which side to take depending on whether she wants to be encouraging or discouraging.

But the bulk of Rafer's job is administrative. The "paperless office" may be theoretically possible using computers and electronic mail systems, but for people in publishing several trees' worth of paper strewn around the office is more typical. Storing mountains of edited material from completed books can be handled by centralized files. The real problem is keeping track of various works in progress. At any one point in time Rafer is responsible for overseeing anywhere from five to ten book manuscripts. Each of these has numerous chapters, and chapters often includes photographs, drawings, and illustrations as well as written material. These chapters go through numerous revisions before they are finally accepted. Keeping track of everything is an enormous job.

Rafer originally thought that her two tables would be sufficient for her work surface needs, but experience has taught her otherwise. These table surfaces are inundated with daily administrative work. A useful storage approach might be a long thin continuous work surface on which she could keep all her "hot files" stored in boxes that range in colors to designate priorities: red for first priority, yellow for second, green for third, then blue and white and such "cooler" colors for pending materials. But Rafer has developed another system. "I'm more comfortable spreading things out while I'm sitting cross-legged on the floor with the manuscript comfortably positioned up on my knees and me sort of sitting leaning against something." It might look funny if you peered through the glass doors, but it works for her.

Using the floor for administrative tasks is a common though haphazard way of handling administrative work. Rather than tossing books and papers on the floor, you might use "kitchen cabinet" tactics: wherever possible, store straw baskets or attractively decorated boxes underneath tables to act as catch-alls. These can be slid under a typewriter table or in a corner to avoid a cluttered look. The floor should never be turned into a last refuge for a harried administrator. It can be used efficiently.

Rafer also needed storage for miscellaneous unfilable papers. She avoided tacking corkboard on the walls because she thought its dark color would make the office dreary. The walls remain an important display surface, however, where she can put up "what pleases me." Some of it is "business" like schedules and phone numbers, but "the rest of it is really fun: postcards, buttons, book covers, ridiculus things I've seen in the newspaper." The walls serve as an icebreaker, especially for people new to the office. But they also serve an important administrative function as a "hanging file." Rather than corkboard, blank stretched canvas is easy to tack things up on, and the white background does not make the wall gloomy. Another way to organize these hanging files is by attaching small pouches to hold invoices and arranging them in columns according to, say, "inside" communications and "out-of-house"items.

The office is a hybrid, part client-centered, part creative, and mostly administrative. Rafer has done a good job zoning it for different activities. Because the editorial side of publishing is closely allied with both clients and creative writing, and in Rafer's own case with art and humor as well, her office reflects characteristics of creative and client-centered offices not usually found in "purer" administrative settings. Client relationships and the imagination required in her editing work have generated a high level of sensitivity to the office environment. Hybrid offices can combine the outstanding qualities of different strains, but they can also result in a workspace that does a little bit of everything without doing anything very well. Sensitive use of activity zoning, body language, and furniture placement and selection help make it work, but this office is overburdened.

MAKING ROOM FOR PEOPLE AMID PAPER

One of the people responsible for New York City's tunnels and bridges operates out of a second type of administrative office. As Assistant Manager, Tunnel and Bridge Facilities for the Port Authority of New York and New Jersey, Alice Herman has an office located in one of the tallest buildings in the world: One World Trade Center. As befits someone in charge of tunnels and bridges, Herman looks out of her window on the seventy-first floor to a vast panorama that includes the Statue of Liberty and dozens of ocean liners sitting like toy ships in the bathtub of New York Harbor far below her. It is a riveting view, that changes hundreds of times a day. It is also a clear indication of her managerial status.

Herman's is a landscaped office, divided from others by partitions that are about four feet high. The offices have no doors. The original intent of office landscaping was to group people together who interact frequently, and to make the lines of communication simple and accessible. In practice, this goal has often not been achieved. Communication is increased, but it is often not the sort that was intended. Social conversations are more likely than work conversations, and concentration privacy is often difficult. But this is not a critical problem for Herman.

Much of her time is spent at the various bridges and tunnels under the Port Authority's jurisdiction, where she is responsible for determining how such matters as toll collection, emergency services, traffic jams, and labor problems can best be handled. The size of her office and the furniture in it—shelves, desk, table—are determined by space standards that allocate such things on the basis of grade level. There is not much choice or flexibility, but this system actually works fairly well.

Herman's storage needs are modest and the shelf space provided is adequate. In fact, Herman's administrative responsibilities center largely around people. Much of her time is spent answering calls from bridge and tunnel workers or meeting with union officials. It is administrative work—constantly collecting and dispensing information and writing reports and memos—but in many ways her office serves analogous functions to client-centered offices, although she does not provide services in the sense that a psychiatrist or attorney does. In fact, conversational privacy and the layout of the office are critical to her administrative function.

The small size of this paper-centered office, which is not fully enclosed, may even contribute to Herman's administrative effectiveness in some subtle and unexpected ways. One way of dealing with the low partitions when conversations are confidential is to lower one's voice. By doing this Herman inadvertently communicates to whomever she is talking with that she is taking them into her special confidence. "It immediately sets a tone of this being a particularly important conversation, or at least removed from general pleasantries." This also creates a climate in which visitors divulge information that they might not otherwise divulge. Psychologists have found that people who communicate their own vulnerability evoke vulnerability on the part of those with whom they are interacting. If I reveal something personal, embarrassing, or confidential to you, you are more likely to let down your guard and reveal something intimate in return. Such information often makes an effective decision possible, and without a doubt it contributes to the mutual trust so important in delicate situations. The possible barrier to effective communication the low partition provides has been turned into an advantage. The same is true of her office's small size.

When Herman meets with visitors in her office, she

finds the smallish size a bonus because it shortens the distance between herself and her visitor. Psychological studies show that people who interact at closer distances associate this with liking and attraction. And if Herman wants more distance, she can move her chair back so that the desk seems a barrier. She does this occasionally when she has a relatively difficult performance appraisal.

Like many administrative offices, this one was not designed to serve any particular purpose well. One of Herman's primary administrative activities is writing reports and memos, which she cannot effectively do in this office during regular working hours. By scheduling her activities in concert with the predictable ebb and flow of people in the office (one of the privacy tools described in Chapter 3) Herman can achieve the level of concentration privacy she needs for this kind of work without taking all if it home. Freedom to come and go depending on her own workstyle makes the office adequate. By understanding how her office affects what she does, and then intelligently managing its use, Herman has made a people place out of what could have been an object place.

MONEY WATCH

Stockbrokers see themselves as a tough, hard-nosed lot, and by and large they live up to their image. Their offices do not fail them in this regard either. For Merrill Lynch research analyst Linda Handloser, the key element in her office is the CRT sitting on the top of her desk. It is her link to the information world. "The most important thing is having a Quotron computer. I was without it for two weeks and felt like a baby without his bottle." With the Quotron on her desk she can talk on the phone and answer a question without missing a beat. From it she gets instantaneous updates on the latest events in financial markets all over the world.

For access to information, office location is nearly as important as the Quotron. Initially Handloser was located far from other research analysts and traders, in what has since become a storage room. "I was out in the boondocks and I felt completely isolated. You just don't have any feel for what's going on." It took her six months to get off her island and onto the information mainland, but the effort was well worth it.

Handloser can call from her office out to a secretary for information, and she can also overhear conversations going on outside her office and contribute information when that is appropriate. For this reason, and because conversational privacy is not important, she rarely works with her door closed. Being near the action has made a tremendous difference to her. "I dreaded coming to work when I was over there in my first office. I was away from everyone, I spent time on the trading floor and didn't necessarily get that much research done."

In summary, the core of an effective administrative office is quick and easy access to people and information. The public image so critical in client-centered offices, and the individual, aesthetic image of creative offices are much less important here, as is the need for communication privacy. The right image for an administrative office is comfortable efficiency—and well-planned storage is a key element of such efficiency. Much of the work is routine, but speeding up routines through organization and use of the right reference tools helps you be a more effective and successful administrator.

WHERE, OH WHERE, DID IT GO?

Most of us caught in an administrative swirl at one time or another have spent a half a day thumbing through endless file drawers, bookshelves, or closets looking for the file, book, or printout that has mysteriously disappeared. You know you had it—yesterday, last week, or a month ago—and you are sure that you did not throw it away, but where is it now? Being able to find information without spending half a day rifling through mountains of paper piled on your desk or in an unorganized filing system, saves you significant time, keeps your blood pressure under control, and helps you look— and be—in control. A good storage system frees an administrator to work *with* information rather than waste time searching for it.

The first step to efficient storage is assessing your own storage needs. What kind of information, and in what form, do you need to get your job done well? Remember that you will have to identify not only what you need to store, but how often you need to retrieve it. Let us look at this self-appraisal process more closely.

Types of Information

Information and other equipment and supplies comes in thousands of shapes and sizes. Before you can intelligently select the appropriate storage system, you need to know the different forms of your own information, supplies, and equipment. Do a detailed inventory, and be specific. Knowing that you handle "paper" is not nearly as useful as knowing that most of that paper is 16 × 20 inches.

Take the time to go through your office and make a written list, first, of what you use in your job. Depending on what you do, this might include:

- paper
- books
- reports
- addresses
- files
- supplies (e.g., paper clips, staples, paper, pencils)
- equipment (e.g., stapler, dictaphone, mat knife, projector)
- drawings and maps
- computer printouts
- journals and magazines
- (extra) chairs, furniture

After you have made this first step, go back through your list and indicate for each item the *most typical* size or shape of it you use and then some of the other sizes or shapes or special characteristics that you sometimes use. Most of the paper you handle may be 8½ × 11 inches, but if there is some that is larger, you had better make note of it—you will have to store it somewhere.

After you have made your initial list, the second step is to indicate on this same list how much of each item you have. Even a gross estimation is useful: lots, some, little. Better, if you have the time, is to try to get a (still rough) estimation of number of feet of books or files or printouts your storage must accommodate, and the general size of storage your equipment requires (e.g., is it about the size of an egg carton or a refrigerator crate?). When this task is completed, you will know how much of each type of storage you need. But there is still one more element to a superefficient storage system.

Activity Rates

Professionals in the field of management of information systems (MIS) talk about "activity rates"—the frequency at which you do certain activities of your job. Do you look at all your files the same number of times in a week, do you use the slide projector every day or once a month, how often do you need to replenish the staple supply? Most of us have some files that we have not looked at for months, others that are integral parts of our working day. Why treat them the same way? If they are "dead" files, why clutter up your immediate workspace? If they are "hot" files, why bury them among files you may never look at again?

For each of the items on your list, indicate roughly what proportion are "hot" and what proportion are "dead." In my own case, I have several file cabinets full of interviews and data analyses from long-completed research projects. In all likelihood, I will never look at them again. They could, for all practical purposes, be stored miles from me, or at least in some central "dead" storage facility. On the other hand, I have files with research articles in them to which I refer constantly in my teaching and current research and writing. Puting these even twenty feet away from my reach would be highly inefficient. In planning your office storage needs, you do not have to provide a place to put everything you have ever used or might use again. All you need is space for what you need *now*.

What Is Available

Now that you know what you must store and retrieve, what kinds of equipment, furniture, and storage systems are best for you? (I will leave out automatic and electronic systems here. They are worth a book in themselves.)

If you need access to information periodically, a flexible, movable storage system may be ideal for you. You also need to think about the size and shape of the space where you work, and fit your storage system to its constraints. There is no point in putting in a large cabinet if there is not sufficient room to open the doors without shoving aside the desk. Here are some characteristics of different storage systems, all readily available from furniture stores, office equipment supply houses, and—with a little ingenuity and work on your part—from hardware stores and thrift shops:

- permanent vs. movable (rolling) units
- sliding, bifold, or swinging doors
- standing or hanging units
- rigid or knockdown units
- short and stackable vs. tall and stand-alone units
- wide vs. narrow shelves
- locking vs. unlockable or open doors
- horizontal vs. vertical file drawers
- finished-back vs. unfinished-back or open shelves.

As you begin to look at different storage ideas, keep these different characteristics in mind. Knockdown cardboard files are excellent if your storage needs are temporary. Modular, stackable units are ideal if you think that your storage needs will be increasing but you do not have the need (or money) to purchase the total system right now. Sliding or bifold doors allow you to put cabinets in narrow spaces where swinging doors are not feasible. If security is a problem, as it is in many open offices, a locking cabinet is critical. Finished-back shelving units that can stand alone or be stacked can be placed within a room to partition space and to create privacy.

- Hallways, corners, and circulation routes are often overlooked storage spaces. Bookshelves can be easily installed using metal standards bought at any hardware store. Files can be sorted into rigid boxlike folders that are more orderly looking than are loose stacks of papers.
- Corkboard glued or nailed or hung from a wall creates vertical space and dampens sound. Tacking things up

in neat rows or in some other obviously planned fashion conveys a sense of order.

Do not waste space under counters or over your head. Vertical dividers can be installed under countertops to create high, thin slots perfect for plans, drawings, and other odd-sized files and supplies. Shelving built in overhead space can be used for storing those things that you rarely need, but that still take up valuable drawer and file space.

With these considerations in mind, as well as information from your earlier storage assessment, you should have a good idea of what kind and how many storage units, and with what characteristics, you need to be able to access and store information efficiently. Things that you use most often should be placed close to you; things less often used, further away.

Storage Strategies

If you have ever worked in a group, you know that time spent clarifying roles and operating procedures is a real time-saver in the long run. The same is true of storage. Take the time to assess your needs and develop a workable system. In the long run, it will save you both time and frustration. Even with the right equipment or furniture you will still need to think about how you are going to use your storage systems. Try color coding. Colored tabs on file folders, for example, with each color corresponding to a category of files, let you see at a glance whether or not a file has been filed correctly. Colors can also indicate "hot" (red or yellow) or "dead" (blue or black) files. Integrated coding systems can be purchased at office-supply stores, or you can develop your own by buying colored self-adhesive tabs in stationery stores.

No matter how diligent you are, over time things are likely to be misfiled or—even more often—no longer needed. Once every six months or once a year, have a personal "ecology day." Go through your files and transfer little-used items from your "hot" to your "dead" files, making way for new things. And realize, as one expert has put it, that "the most effective way to reduce records cost is not to create it." If you do not need it, get rid of it.

CHAPTER SEVEN

The Client-Oriented Office

More than the creative office, where the rule is originality, or the administrative office, which favors efficiency, the client-centered office is 99 percent image. If a large part of your business involves client contact, start thinking of your office as a mirror image of your ideal self—because you will want the client to see you at your total best. Depending on your profession, your "best" will mean projecting an image of equalizing friendliness, of no-nonsense professionalism, of nurturing calm and security, or of a rousing display of originality and creative insight. The workspaces profiled in this chapter show how to emphasize one image over another, depending on the image you choose to project.

The thing to remember is that all client-centered offices have two features in common: comfort and communication privacy. First, what does comfort involve? Your goal, if you see many clients, is to make your visitor feel "at home." This is not comfort for comfort's sake, however. In the client-centered office, *your power is proportional to your client's comfort and privacy*. Why?

To provide effective services, whether legal, financial, therapeutic, educational, or sales, you need to know your client. Comfort reduces tension, undermines defenses, strips pretense.

The second element, communication privacy, eliminates the fear of being overheard and so minimizes embarrassment and ego-threatening personal vulnerability. Whether you are a lawyer, therapist, manager, or professor the quality of the advice and guidance you provide depends on the free flow of information and ideas. In a sense, communication privacy is a form of comfort. It can act as a catalyst that stimulates effective communication. Offices that are both comfortable and private help people reveal themselves.

One caveat: Though you want to learn as much as possible about your client, customer, or patient, you do not want to give away very much information about yourself. You will want to come across as concerned, human, and friendly. But you also need to maintain some distance. A razor's edge stands between becoming too personal and familiar and remaining too institutional and distant.

How much of yourself you reveal in your client-centered office will vary with your profession and business. But the rule of thumb is to be personable and comfortable without becoming intimate. How to communicate these traits through your office design revolves around the specific kinds of environmental supports and cues that you bring in—and leave out—of the office, whether it be furniture brought from home to give a warm "living-room" feel to your office, or the omission of family photos and momentos that may typecast you badly in a client's eyes. Even more than other offices, the client-centered office is a compromise. It represents a part, but not the whole, of who you are.

If you are in a service profession, as a therapist is, the goal is to create a comfortable but neutral space—one that is not especially interesting, fun, or unusual. The idea is to present an essentially blank page onto which the client can project his or her own feelings without filtering them first. Physical cues in the office should not create expectations that limit or block clients from expressing their attitudes and thoughts.

A creative business such as advertising should achieve the opposite goal. You want your office to say, "Look, we're different here." Or if you need to inspire accessibility, as a professor does, you will want a comfortable office with softer seating that can be arranged informally around small tables to stimulate interaction. And if you are an attorney or accountant you may need to draw the line between projecting an image that is personal and one that is intimate because some facets of your life would interfere with your business. Clues about religious preference or political persuasion may attract some clients but will alienate many others. More is likely to be lost than gained by such displays.

Finally, the good client-centered office also communicates confidence and control through clearly structured and comfortable seating arrangements. You should not have to scramble and search for a chair every time a visitor comes in. Let your clients know where to sit or wait with furniture arrangements such as corner-to-corner seating or chairs at a coffee or small conference table. Once you sit down, there should be one or two obvious places where your clients can choose to sit. Where they choose to sit gives you a cue to their comfort (the further away from you, the more uncomfortable, anxious, or wary they are). Giving clients a limited choice contributes positively to their comfort by telling them, nonverbally, that you are not trying to completely control or regiment them.

Comfortable seating arrangements, communication privacy, icebreakers that are personal but not intimate, visually pleasing and interesting fabrics and colors, and comfortable nonuniform lighting create the impression that you have thought and care a great deal about your clients' needs. Power in the client-centered office means establishing this kind of effective interpersonal communication.

IMPRESSING WITH FRIENDLINESS

The War Between the Tates was not written here, but this office is where author Alison Lurie does all kinds of academic business as a professor of English. She does not write in her university office because people can "come knock on the door and ask for a copy of tomorrow's assignment or call me up." It is not private and it does not work for her as a creative office. It works very well, however, as a client-centered office. Students are the clients.

When Lurie moved into the office the walls were lined from floor to ceiling with bookshelves—too many of them, in fact. The first thing Lurie did was to remove several of the bottom shelves. She did not need that much space for storage, and she could use it instead for tables and other working surfaces.

The effect Lurie was striving for was hominess, which she achieved by eliminating some storage space and by bringing in plants and her own furniture from home, including a small oriental rug, an old easy chair, and several wicker chairs arranged around a small coffee table. They created what is, in fact, very much a sitting-room atmosphere. "I don't feel comfortable working in a cold and sterile institutional setting, and I want the students who come here to feel comfortable. I don't want them to feel as though they are dealing entirely with an official."

Interestingly, the aesthetic effect of most storage furnishings tends toward the cold and institutional. Instead of filling an office with boxes and file cabinets and more shelving units, unusual items like wicker baskets or pegboard displays double as storage and as aesthetically pleasing art-forms besides.

The warmth and informality of Lurie's furniture is enhanced by the way she has arranged it. "I want to encourage the students to sit down at the coffee table rather than to face me across a desk." Whenever someone comes in to see her, she moves from her desk, if she is working there, to sit at the coffee table with them. The particular seat she takes depends on where the student sits. Lurie always wants to sit next to the student because she does not want "to be confronting them across a surface." If she is sitting at the coffee table before the student comes in, Lurie typically sits in the green easy chair. "This is the best chair. It's the most comfortable chair, and it's the chair I sit in if I want to read." If a student comes in and sits at a chair across the coffee table from her, she will ask the student to move to a chair next to her "so we can look at whatever it is we're looking at."

The green easy chair works well for a different reason also. When sitting in it, Lurie is several inches lower than anyone sitting in the other chairs. For people with fragile status and authority, sitting in such a chair would be inadvisable; they would appear weaker and less confident than they actually are. This is not Lurie's problem. Lurie is well known and respected, and if anything people are intimidated by meeting with a well-known writer on a one-to-one basis. By sitting in a lower chair Lurie maintains not only her own comfort, she also puts her guests at ease.

Two of the visitor's chairs are old wicker chairs that she bought second-hand in Los Angeles about twenty years ago. The beauty of wicker chairs is that they are extremely comfortable without being totally relaxing. They are perfect for putting visitors at ease without making them so relaxed that the purpose of the meeting is lost.

Lurie also wants visitors "to feel that I am sympathetic and informal, and *that I have a lot of different interests*." A touch that helps set her off from the majority of her colleagues is a series of student photographs on the wall near the coffee table. "The most eccentric thing in this office is the gallery of former students. I began it about a

Comfortable and homelike chairs arranged around a coffee table help writer and professor Alison Lurie, author of The War Between the Tates *and more recently* The Language of Clothes, *present sides of her personality that do not readily appear in the more formal classroom. The photo gallery of former students lining one wall helps Lurie connect names, faces, and records when former students write asking for recommendations. It is a potent environmental message, silently communicating Lurie's interest in her students and others with whom she deals.*

year after I started to teach here, and I continue to take photographs of all my classes." The photographs help her remember the individuals for whom she may need to write a recommendation. But because students also like to "look for their friends," the photos serve an additional function as icebreakers.

As a particular type of client-centered office, this one works very effectively. Lurie's office is intended to mini-mize hierarchy and to restructure the well-defined roles of student-professor or leader-follower. Lurie does not want to hold a tight rein on the interaction; she values her clients—or students—for their spontaneity. This type of interaction also serves well other professions where meetings serve as idea and activity producers, as marketing people, sales people and others have found.

Since so much of our role behavior is place-specific, the nonhierarchical office can aid people in shedding stereotyped role behavior. Nonhierarchical elements are informal circular seating arrangements and comfortable chairs. Lurie could have plastered the walls with press clippings and book covers, but this would create distance and reinforce hierarchy—the antithesis of a good client-centered office for what she wants to achieve. In another client-centered office such as a lawyer's or dentist's, the nature of the client relationship is different, and the primary functions the office serves also would find the impression of friendliness out of place.

EMPHASIS ON PROFESSIONALISM

I met Julian Steiner at his law office. We talked for a while, grabbed a bite to eat, and then hailed a taxi and drove to his dental office. He shed his coat and put on a dental jacket, and I was looking at a different person in a completely different office environment. In both, however, even a stranger would have identified Steiner as the professional par excellence—the man in charge.

Steiner had practiced dentistry for a number of years but then suffered a boating accident in which he hurt his back and required serious back surgery. It then became clear that Steiner would have to find another source of income because he would be unable to practice "chair-side dentistry" full time. For many, this would have been a severe blow. Steiner rolled with the punch, ended up in law school, and eventually made his specialty medical malpractice.

Given the two very different professions of law and dentistry, I was fascinated by what the two offices would look like. I was not disappointed. At the law office, the overall color scheme is slate gray and subdued in tone. In contrast, the reception area and conference room are "jet black, high luster, and chromium yellow." This is unusual for a law office and, as Steiner notes, definitely not "at-ease putting." It is deliberate, however, The partners wanted a "handsome space that is very sleek, modern, and forward-looking—not one that reassures you, as some of the older, handsome oriental-carpeted offices do. This room shows that "we are in business and will get the most for you that we possibly can." Steiner is not particularly comfortable with this bedazzling, hard-edged image, but it makes sense to him. "We are also not one of those old-time law offices that have accrued a kind of serenity." He contrasts the law office's up-to-the-minute image to "old-time banks that can afford to waste space and display handsome vaults and old-fashioned cashier booths with the brash youngster who comes in and wants to prove he is all business and efficiency."

Steiner designed his own office in striking contrast to the surrounding rooms. "My office has oriental carpets, a lot of furniture from my home, and some of my paintings." Why? "The office is my microenvironment. While clients can be jarred as much as they care to be outside, when they come to my office, the impression I want them to have is one of confidence and assuredness—quality but without pressure." These functional "living room" furnishings create an atmosphere that is personal without being intimate. "In my law office there is no reason why anyone should know anything about my personal existence unless I choose to tell them, in which case I can do it verbally." For these reasons he is willing to bring in furniture and paintings that express his own values and his own way of dealing with his clients, but he is not willing to bring in pictures of his family or other aspects of his personal life. Portraits of yourself and others invite comment. Unless they are of clients (like Alison Lurie's) you are better off without them in a client-centered office if you would rather not be the subject of discussion.

In Steiner's law offices accessibility is much less important than convincing the potential client to become an actual one. The role relationship here tends more toward the formal than it did in Lurie's office. Steiner's oriental carpets and expensive furniture are unfailing status and financial cues even though they project a more personal living-room atmosphere. Steiner's aim here is to create a climate of trust. Ironically, the real benefit of this may accrue when cases are lost. Steiner's clients may be more likely to feel that he has done a good job—win or lose—because of the more personal relationship his office will help him establish. In an expensive but less personal office it is easier for clients to feel that the attorney did not give his all because there was not enough money in it or because he was too busy handling other cases needed to support an obviously recent and expensive workstyle.

Dentist Steiner wants to convey a very different image to clients. Here, the patient is often "terrified by dentistry." Because the client is uncomfortable and anxious, "he needs to be reassured that the dentist is someone he knows, trusts, and has some commonality with. He has to be a little more at ease. There's no need for that at the law office." Not only is no pain going to be inflicted on his law clients, but typically people come to lawyers as plaintiffs who are initiating suit; the whole dynamic is very different. But in other offices, at a banker's or at a doctor's or therapist's office, reassurance is vital.

Steiner and his associate have done a very good job of creating a dental office that is reassuring and comfortable. The reception room is large and comfortable, with soft low light provided by lamps rather than by overhead fluorescent fixtures. On one wall is a folksy, fascinating display of antique dental artifacts. The display reveals Steiner's interest in antiques and in the history of dentistry that intrigue the client without communicating anything about the doctor's more personal life. The room seems unstaged and unpretentious. Neither the furniture nor the paintings are expensive or noteworthy. The room works for just these reasons. It seems to say, effortlessly, "I'll be with you in a minute. Make yourself comfortable. There's nothing to worry about." Yet if this were all it communicated, this office would fail.

The waiting room in Steiner's dental office suits its purpose perfectly. Low lighting, comfortable but unimposing furniture, and a fascinating display of antique dental artifacts combine to produce a space that is calm and reassuring without being boring and institutional. It is in direct contrast to the efficiency and professionalism projected by the examination room.

We want doctors' and dentists' offices to be friendly and their waiting rooms to be homey, but we also look for no-nonsense signs that our ills will be treated with the most modern medical equipment and practices. Homey does not convey a strong sense of up-to-the minute professionalism. That is why two distinct spatial zones exist in Steiner's dental office.

When the client crosses the threshold from the waiting room into the actual examination area the whole atmosphere changes. The lighting is much brighter and the surfaces are white and hard. This atmosphere is reinforced by a wall filled with diplomas and certificates. "When you're in the outside room, sitting and reading and relaxing while you're waiting for your appointment, you don't have to be confronted with that professional theme." But once you have crossed the threshold, you are confronted with it and it acts as a device for cueing both dentist and patient about what is expected in this area. It is as appropriate and effective for its function as the outer office is for reassurance.

It is possible to create this "duo-toned" sense in any office where calm should not obscure professionalism. Most useful is a zoned seating area that is comfortable and personal and distinct from a desk or workspace, which is where diplomas and awards might be confined. You can separate these zones best by lighting up the desk area with a white light fixture and light down the seating area, which might simply be two chairs around a small table and facing into a corner.

FISHBOWL SECURITY

Like many therapists, Carol Skinner's approach to patients and to her office design is eclectic. "I use different things for different people." She tries to create a situation in which patients can explore and bring to the surface those memories and emotions that are most important to them. And she has succeeded. Skinner "loves space" and is obviously sensitive to how it can be organized to make her as effective as possible.

Skinner's office is in a new wing of a building, and its most striking characteristic is the glass that runs from floor to ceiling on two sides. Skinner was able to choose the office, and did so because of the charming gorge with little stream and falls that appears outside the window, but she is always concerned about the glass and the absence of privacy it creates. She knew that a "glass cage" was "totally antithetical to the needs of a therapist's office. You really want people to feel private and to feel that their visits are confidential." People know that this is a place where they can be comfortable and supported and that the therapist is an ally with whom they are working together. So many people today find themselves in "fishbowl" offices either surrounded by glass walls or by no walls, just space. Yet in studying how Skinner arranged her office to minimize this negative effect tells us—whatever our profession—how to accommodate clients in a problematic atmosphere.

Before moving into the office Skinner would come in and try standing and sitting in different places in the office to see the effect from each of them. It helped her decide that "I didn't want to have curtains because it seems like such a contradiction of terms to have this glorious outside and cover it with curtains, but I wanted to be sure the client felt secure in here." In some glass-walled offices, curtains are not permitted. But Skinner's solution was to put the client's chair in the corner, looking away from the windows, where the two glass walls met. She also placed tall plants all around the window on the floor rather than hanging them as she might have done in another office. The "plant screen" around the bottom made the office private and still left it "permeable" to the outside. By putting clients in this screened corner so that they faced away from the windows into the solid parts of the office, Skinner was able to maximize their sense of enclosure and protection. The combination of this orientation and the fact that once clients start talking "they tend to be pretty oblivious to surroundings, except in a subliminal way" has allowed Skinner to achieve protection for her clients without sacrificing her own need for a comfortable, stimulating office.

Therapist Carol Skinner created visual privacy by placing plants around the bottom of the floor-to-ceiling window walls where they block the view of passers-by without eliminating natural light or her view of a small gorge with trees and a running brook. Skinner further enhanced patients' sense of being visually protected by locating the patient's chair in the corner where the two window walls meet, so that the patient is looking at solid walls. The overall effect is pleasant, comfortable, and private.

Skinner's own comfort is not a minor point, nor should it be for anyone who spends long hours in an office. A pleasant view keeps Skinner fresh and helps replenish the enormous energy her job requires. The change in perspective offered by the view is restful. "It's not that it takes my focus away, I can still focus on exactly what the client is saying, but it keeps me sane." She has worked in windowless offices before and found them "terrible. It's worse for me than the clients, because they only come for an hour." If she had not had such a gorgeous view, then a quick walk outdoors, or even a radio playing very quietly in the background between clients' visits would have offered a helpful "escape."

You should always be aware that a comfortable office is not a perquisite, but a necessity if you are to do your job well. Studies of nonverbal communication show that we express our feelings and attitudes subtly and unintentionally. Tension can be expressed in slightly greater irritableness, an eyebrow that says I am tired, an extra few glances out the window, or more frequent shifting of positions. All communicate a restleness that may be misinterpreted by a client as boredom.

Similarly, making a client comfortable is critical to Skinner's effectiveness. Skinner does not have a couch, because she prefers a reclining chair. Unlike the analytical arrangement in which the therapist always sits out of sight, behind the patient, she sits directly facing the client. When she has more than one person in therapy, as in dealing with couples or even whole families, she likes a "triangular arrangement because I want the couple to be able to talk to each other and also to me and to have our relationship be like an equilateral triangle of which I'm a part but not the focus."

Her wall decorations too were brought in—from home—not just because their colors match or their shapes are interesting, but because they convey silent messages to clients. The drawings directly connect to her life and her image of herself as a therapist. "This is Rembrandt, a mother carrying her child. This one is a Picasso. It is a woman holding a mirror for another woman to look at herself in. That's exactly what I'm doing, whether for a man or a woman." The third drawing, by Dürer, depicts a rabbit. "It's soft and furry. These three pictures expressed my sense of nurturing"—essential given the "painful process" of therapy.

So while the office has some relatively abstract cues to Skinner's own personal life and values, it is not at all revealing of who she is outside the office. "I would not have pictures of my children or a family member or of anybody who means something to me because I don't want to have so specific an image that people won't talk about certain things because they feel I'll have a certain type of response." When cues given by personal objects and momentos are overly personal, the result can be defensiveness on the client's part.

There is little to distract the client here. The colors are neutral and the walls are relatively blank. By having her clients sit in the corner facing these relatively neutral walls, Skinner has them focus their attention on her while momentarily shifting their gaze to one of the other drawings, the plants, or even outside. In a different kind of office, such a design would be too bland, but it works for Skinner—and would work for anyone for whom communication privacy was an important feature.

Conveying an Image of Creativity

Whereas a medical waiting room is meant to reassure and relax, a professor's office to equalize and democratize, a lawyer's office or medical examination room to create confidence in the expert's capabilities, and a therapist's office to provide a neutral background against which volatile emotions are played out—a good advertising office stimulates, excites, energizes, and animates its clients. From moon posters on ceilings, supergraphics on walls, rock music, and beer in the coke machine to busts of Abraham Lincoln and black walls in the conference room, J. B. Graves's office is designed to put some zing and snap into clients' lives. Privacy is much less important here than in an attorney's or a therapist's office. The bland neutrality or sense of decorum that is so appropriate to these types of client-centered offices would be totally counterproductive here.

When Graves decided to start his own agency, he named it HourAgency to reflect a basic underlying philosophy: Everybody who works at the firm is part-of the firm. "I didn't want the paycheck to do all the talking." Equity positions are held by anyone who has been there for a certain period of time. "People are given stock. They own the company." Graves organized the HourAgency this way because he had not felt like a part of the business in any of his other jobs. He had been only a worker, which had not been satisfying.

Graves's own office is deliberately planned to help him function creatively as leader and guiding light of the agency, even to sacrificing whatever he might personally find most comfortable. "I like my privacy, but I have sacrificed that privacy to be aware of what's going on. I like to be in the center of things." His office is command central. Upon entering on the ground floor into a reception area you can look up about a half flight of stairs through an opening and see into an office that has a huge mural of the earth on the ceiling. This is Graves' office, smack in the center of the whole operation.

"Accessibility is a very big thing. Everybody needs a leader. Whether I'm the best one or not doesn't matter if I'm the guy people—clients or employees—can turn to." Graves once had an office in the back of the building but there was not enough contact so people were always curious about what he was doing back there. Was he sleeping, eating, seeing a secretary? They did not know, and the kind of openness and vitality he wanted did not occur.

But contact of just any sort would not do. Graves tries to make the agency fun because he thinks that people do not work well in an awful place. He wants the office to be open and lively, but different from the openness of landscaped settings. "Here there are doors, but they are open. People have an option. They can close doors if they want to, but they elect never to do it." This kind of environment does more than motivate people once they are here. It is a recruitment tool. "I use this environment to buy good help. It's part of my fringe benefits. I get very good people because they walk in here and they like it."

Graves is trying, and largely succeeding, to get the best out of two worlds. "If the working environment has got the razor's edge between austerity and sickening sensuousness, then you're going to get the best of both worlds." He has given his employees creative freedom in their work. Instead of installing a central music system, for example, he has bought people their own radios, and even small televisions. "Whatever you want in your own place but no elevator music." He realized that "no matter how small the company is, if there are more than two, they are marching to different drummers at different times of the day." Real productivity comes from letting the bands march on rather than trying to put up barricades.

In his own office most of the things were put there for a specific reason. Graves has positioned his desk so that the light from his window falls over his side. He prefers this to sitting in front of a large window, which puts his own face in dark shadows while putting the visitor's in total light, but also at the same time making the visitor very uncomfortable as he or she tries unsuccessfully to read the cues from his face. Graves uses the sliver of light to his side to shade his face while lighting up his clients' faces. "I can watch you when you are honest with me or when you are a little nervous. I can really see all that stuff without blinding you."

Even the objects that he has put on the shelves have a purpose. Graves does not see himself as any less a creative person than a businessman, and the light bulbs on the shelf behind his desk symbolize the creative part of his personality. He keeps them there for their symbolic value. He also sees himself as a family man and so he has pictures of his children on the shelf—the intent is a total image. "Everything is just designed to make it as comfortable and human a business atmosphere as I can make it." He has succeeded.

In his own office as well as in the office complex, Graves has walked a tightrope between being personal and intimate, between being institutional and homey, between being soft and productive. It works because he has been able to separate the positive aspects of comfort and the need to accommodate individual differences from a rigid attempt to maintain a single "party line." Graves could totally control the situation, but he knows that his real power lies in his creating an elastic framework within which others are free to express themselves. His office complex works as a client-centered office because the benefits to those working there are communicated to clients and visitors in hundreds of subtle ways: genuine smiles, lack of tension in the air and comfortable conversations.

The purpose of this kind of office is not to demonstrate sympathy or financial success but rather creativity, innovativeness, and fun. The image of creativity works well with clients, who are there to buy the agency's art. The creative benefits available to employees are communicated to clients via the staffers' sense of dedicated fun.

From pure visual interest to its imposing symbolism ("We're out of the world here"), this kind of huge poster, hung on the ceiling, communicates the impression of fun and innovation that J. B. Graves wants his office to convey.

SUMMARY

Each of these client-centered offices is different from the others. What unifies them all is that, for their respective clients, they create confidence. Privacy, power, status, and personalization are balanced, keeping constantly in mind the particular clientele to which each is directed. These offices are powerful because they work to facilitate appropriate kinds of interpersonal interaction. This is what, above all else, a client-centered office is about.

CHAPTER EIGHT

The Home Office

Refuge, hideaway, personal retreat, castle, womb, sanctuary. The home is some of these things, some of the time. It is also word-processing center, executive suite, open office, and communications center. More and more of us are working at home, part-time and full-time, during the day and at night, on the weekends and over holidays. Second offices are more common than second homes.

For your home to become an effective office it cannot sacrifice its value as a home, but it must provide the cues you need to work. We know who we are by where we are. As one working woman put it, "Every morning as I neared my office—as I put more blocks between myself and home—I felt the layers of housewife peeling off."

Status, power, and privacy are important factors to consider. But so are more basic things. If you work at home, you need space to concentrate, to communicate with clients and customers, and to store efficiently any materials you need to get the job done. You also need to consider your family's requirements as well. Their desire for access to you, for using the home as a "backstage" area where they do not have to maintain public faces, where they can be messy, dress in jeans, and yell at each other. Walking this tightrope and balancing your competing interests, requirements, and loyalties—to say nothing of the lure of refrigerator, stereo, or TV—can be the ultimate test of your people skills, motivation, and patience. A well-planned home office can make the difference between an aggravating, tension-producing, and unproductive work experience and one that is satisfying and productive. How can you rethink your home workspace to avoid the pitfalls and maximize the ease commuters can only dream about?

TYPES OF HOMEWORK

The success of your home as an office depends in part upon the kind of work you try to do there. Many people use the home as a cocoon. It is the one place where you are least likely to suffer distractions and interruptions. "Burning the midnight oil" or being up at "the crack of dawn" usually occur at home. Beds, couches, hammocks, and chaise lounges are as likely locations for setting up shop as the dining-room table or the desk in the den.

Home offices can be overflow tanks for people with main offices outside the home. If you are at your peak during the normal working day, you are more likely to save busy-work for home: signing forms, simple correspondence, charting the next day's plan of attack, making "to do" lists, light reading. But for free-lancers and the self-employed, the home is not the "other" place, but corporate headquarters. It is the store, warehouse, and administrative center rolled into a corner.

Where do you do work at home? Dining room, bathroom, bedroom, study, all-purpose room? Are you alone? Where are the kids? Where is your husband or wife? What is your family doing? Before you trade in the office downtown for work at home, you need to answer these questions.

SHARED *vs.* EXCLUSIVE SPACE

Many home-workers would love to have their own exclusive space. The economics of an extra room can make this impossible, but you need not despair. For some surprising reasons a shared space may be better, especially if you have young children.

Researcher Mary Ann McLaughlin found that women who work at home in either sales or office-type jobs were able to work more effectively when they had shared rather than exclusive space. Exclusive space was defined as an area reserved solely for your own work. You do not have to constantly put away typewriter, order forms, and all the other paraphernalia of whatever you are doing so that someone else can use the same space for a different purpose. Shared space was defined as a work area used by others in the family for their own activity: people eating in the dining room while you are trying to complete order forms or receive business calls, trying to sleep while you use the computer terminal, or playing Monopoly in the den when you are trying to read technical reports. We had expected that people with exclusive space would experience fewer interruptions and would be more productive. So much for hypotheses. Why was the opposite true?

While many of the home-workers McLaughlin studied had "exclusive" space, it was often blue-finger space: located in damp and unheated basements, underheated porches, and spare rooms. Leftover space. Those who had exclusive space often did not use it except as storage for their work materials. They really worked in the dining room, or elsewhere, only darting in and out of their storage area.

The problem was psychological. Home-workers with exclusive space had expectations of being able to work without distractions. Physical boundaries between work and nonwork were strong, and they expected to be able to keep the two domains separate. People who worked in shared spaces, on the other hand, had no false illusions. They expected to be interrupted. They knew, because of their vulnerable locations, that their children would roam in and out asking for peanut butter sandwiches or wanting to know whether they could watch television. McLaughlin found that the experience of interference was a function of expectations. *If you do not expect to be bothered and find that you are interrupted, you are more likely to be irritated, and to experience interruptions more strongly, than if you have few expectations about interruptions.*

If, therefore, you have young children or others at home, you would do better to stake out a corner of the dining room as your own than to find less than adequate "exclusive space." Shelving units with drawers, a fold-out writing surface, and cabinet doors can be closed up on a minute's notice to shut from view the ordered disarray of your working life. These units comfortably fit in most dining rooms, and they look like dining-room furniture. If you can work only in the kitchen, try to zone a small part of it just for work. Take one or two drawers and use them for writing materials, pads, order forms, "must" references. Try doing the same for a part of the kitchen counter. Build a little boundary line by gluing something like a thin piece of one-inch-high wooden molding (bought at any hardware store) to indicate where your "office" starts and the kitchen counter ends.

Exclusive space is essential, however, when working at home threatens shaky professional identities. People who do not have strong ties to well-established organizations, who are trying to start small businesses of their own, or who are working on a free-lance basis may have a fragile self-image as a professional. Husbands or wives, children, friends, or neighbors may not take them seriously. Yes, they know that they are working. But the attitude can be that it is just a temporary sideline, something to do to make a little extra money, to help the time pass now that the children are older. Nothing serious. Certainly not a career. One friend we know, who is in real estate, had gone to the trouble of putting a formal nameplate on the door of her home study to underscore her professional identity.

Thus the value of exclusive space *in a desirable location* is that it reinforces the value of one's work to oneself as well as to others. Working out of the corner closet or the back of the basement does not do much to support your professional image. If you are serious about your work, try to stake out some territory in the home that can be treated as a separate work zone. A designated corner of the bedroom or dining room, marked by a small desk and some storage or a screen is a step in the right direction. The more exclusive your space, the better.

Family and friends will begin to treat your work zone like an office. They are less likely to disturb you when you are working there than if you work sitting on the living room couch or at the kitchen table.

HOME OFFICE: FRONTSTAGE OR BACKSTAGE

Many kinds of work generate debris—everything from empty packing boxes to computer printouts. It may sound like a small problem, but many people associate a "messy" house with an unsuccessful housekeeper. Stacks of computer printouts strung around the bedroom can irritate like salt in a raw wound.

You need to think about more than where the computer console will go. What about printouts and old research files? Cold, out-of-the-way rooms unsuitable for work may be perfect for storing work debris. Section off a part of the basement or garage for your dead files, and reserve part of the bookshelves or kitchen cabinets for your hot files. If space is at a real premium in the more public parts of your apartment or house, try using a "work tray." This could be a table on wheels, or a rectangular piece of wood about the width of your counter with edges around the sides and some kind of sturdy handle that makes it easy to pick up and move from place to place. When you are working, take it from the back room and set it on the counter. When you are through, cart it back to its storage place. The beauty is that you do not have to totally unpack and reorganize all the pieces of your work each time you start or stop. It is a mobile exclusive space.

The importance of maintaining a clean image is even greater when your work at home requires visits by clients or customers. In one study we found that people started to treat their home, which is generally a backstage area where they can retreat and let down their hair, as a frontstage area. One woman required her children to keep their rooms neater than she herself felt was necessary because her customers often came to the house and wanted to look around. She ended up buying a dishwasher into which she could dump dirty dishes quickly.

MOTIVATION

Children are by no means the only source of distraction at home. Many of us are self-interrupters. With or without children the refrigerator, television, stereo, laundry, and even dirty dishes may invite us down wayward paths.

The extent to which the activity and excitement of the office environment acts as a motivator was revealed by one stockbroker who psyched himself up for the working at home by getting up in the morning and, after showering and shaving, proceded to put on his three-piece suit and to play a recording of the sounds of the office. With all these cues he was able to get in the mood to work.

Jane Geniesse, a free-lance writer, has written about the distractions that lie in wait. "If you work at home, there are distractions. One stumbles over them like boulders in the path of efficiency. One is vulnerable to the telephone, a long-winded superintendent, a child home sick. The unexpected constantly gets you by the jugular. As a friend of mine said, 'Working at home is a cat's paw on a beautifully drafted drawing.'" Every time Geniesse looks up she sees things that need to be done: laundry, dishes, cleaning of all sorts. It takes an act of will to resist cleaning up and stick with the work at hand.

Women seem to find it harder to ignore these kinds of daily chores than men—not because women are naturally attracted to such drudgery, but because for many of them cleaning and keeping house have fallen, largely by default, into their hands. When women work at home, the homework is often just added to the housework. Where all this energy is supposed to come from is not clear.

Finding a place to work that is out of sight of temptations will help. You may also find that, like the stockbroker, you need to bring into your home workspace elements of the "office" that act as a constant reminder of your professional role. Expensive equipment like typewriters, telephone answering machines, and computers can motivate because they say, "You bought me, now work to pay for me." Changing from your pajamas into a suit sounds extreme, but clothes help us as well as others to know who we are, and our own behavior will "firm up" in more formal clothes.

But there are other elements beyond a design-wise office that are essential to home-workers. According to Geniesse, home-workers "must be immune to distractions, they must be their own self-starters with internalized time clocks. They must steel themselves to sound professional even though the laundry is being delivered when they have finally gotten to interview Senator Javits on the telephone." Working at home can also be lonely.

Leave the house when you start to go stir-crazy with cabin fever. If what you need is more a faint hum of activity than real conversations, try working at a public library for a brief part of the day. A library is a good place for research, writing, and thinking. Drop in at your editor's or the local sales office. Arrange your day so that it has a pattern. Work at home in the morning, roam during the early afternoon, get back to work in the late afternoon. If you actively seek people-contact when you need it, your home office will feel more like a refuge than a prison.

TRANSITIONS

One of the values of separating work life and home life is the ability to unwind on the way home and wind up again in the morning. Having a separate room or even a special chair to go to when you get home, which children, spouse, or housemates know is off-limits, creates a transition time that can do much to reduce tensions in many families. Even how you get to and from work can be important. When I ride my bicycle to work, I am in a much better frame of mind and am more accessible to everyone the minute I walk in the door than when I drive. The exercise and fresh air are energizing, and the extra time gives me a chance to go over and reflect on the day's events. Four walls and a door is not the only place for contemplation privacy! By the time I get home, I am ready to see everyone. Bicycling is not for everyone, but walking is. Try deliberately parking your car further away than usual and walking partway to work. Even bus and subway rides can be made more pleasant if you get off before your closest stop and walk partway.

Anyone working at home part-time or full-time confronts these basic issues. How, specifically, have an author, artist, architect, and psychiatrist solved the problems of working at home through savvy office arrangements? Their solutions may not be your own, but they will give you some good ideas.

BACKSTAGE ACCLAIM

Joan Kron is one of the most wide-ranging and respected commentators on interior design in America today. She is one of those rare people who fully appreciate the aesthetic aspects of design without losing sight of its ultimate goal as a backdrop and support. From her hugely successful book *High Tech* (which she co-authored) to a landmark story on hospices—(hospitals for the terminally ill)—Kron has perceptively written about what design not only is but could be. She has done this as a senior editor for *New York Magazine,* as a chief reporter of the Home Section of the *New York Times,* and as the author of dozens of articles.

Kron needs access to information and an environment where she can comfortably write. In order to be able to

Joan Kron's home office is a private creative space, designed to support her own workstyle, not to impress visitors. A long counter that supports collapsable cardboard file boxes is a perfect way to keep manuscript material open, accessible, and orderly. Wire storage bins attached to wall shelving units generate even more usable storage space.

devote full time to *High Tech,* Kron quit her job at the *New York Times* and started working entirely at home. From simple but effective storage systems to a sophisticated electronic word processor, hard copy printer, and photocopying machine, her home office has what it takes to be a useful tool of her trade.

One room of a three-bedroom apartment is the primary workspace. For day-to-day work this room is the "brains of the house." When Kron was working on *High*

This separate work zone has been carved out of an entrance area and is used for handling administrative and financial details, and making phone calls. Working here, Kron can see into the living room whose southern exposure captures welcome sunlight and provides a change of pace from her more private study.

Tech, it remained the nerve center, but the whole apartment became the office, including the dining room, a small work area right off the entrance, and the living room. A tolerant husband and no children at home made this possible. It is in her own room, however, where she maintains her extensive library and does most of her writing.

Storage is always a problem, but Kron has put her own high-tech ideas to work. Simple shelves line both walls, and from these shelves hang wire baskets from which she can easily keep separate the various parts of the manuscripts she is working on. Long thin counters hold simple knock-down cardboard file boxes, each of which contains different chapters. Everything is right at hand, and new material can be added easily.

The office's only drawback is that it faces north and does not get much sunlight. Natural light is important to her, so Kron does some of her work at a built-in counter near the apartment entrance. From here she can look into the living room, whose southern exposure lets light stream in during the day. This entrance area is zoned mostly for personal correspondence and bookkeeping; which she likes to keep separate from her writing.

Although her office was designed with the help of an architect and works quite well, Kron continually makes small changes to increase its efficiency and effectiveness. For example, she is now dissatisfied with the lack of surface area near her word processor. Because the processor needs a special electrical outlet, she is unable to move it around to get the L-shaped arrangement that would work best for her. But rather than just suffering the inconvenience, she is getting a big table and a swivel chair so that she can move along the length of the table as she is working.

The apartment and her own work space were deliberately designed to project a high-tech image. But the hard-edged, impersonal, unused impression that high tech can convey is here tempered by a comfortableness that comes with good use. The high-tech storage system composed of wire and cardboard boxes holds material that she uses all the time. Constantly opening and closing file drawers would be a major inconvenience. The file system Kron has developed may look messy to an outsider, but in fact it is highly efficient, and visitors rarely tour this backstage area anyway. Kron knows what she has and where she is on a manuscript at a glance, and she can add new information quickly to her files.

Is Kron's home office perfect? Of course not, but it has helped her fully enjoy her extended sabbatical from regular employment, though Kron is eager to get back to work in a "regular" job. Working without interruptions is a great boon to her creativity, but she misses not being connected to other people and finds that work over a long period at home can be boring and tedious. In general, Kron's home office reflects a humanistic application of high tech's principles. It is flexible and relatively inexpensive. Its value lies in the ability to help Kron work effectively. Essentially her work area is a backstage zone not intended for the casual visitor. The opportunity to have a private office allows her to maintain the living area as a more public frontstage area in which she can entertain her many friends and visitors. The concept of zoning becomes even more critical in a home office that must accommodate work involving clients. We turn to such an office next.

FRONTSTAGE SPOTLIGHT

Contrary to what you might think, the need for zoning your space in clear-cut ways is not lessened if you live alone. Public and private selves should still remain separate. But with the space and autonomy you gain from living alone, public spaces may be zoned for much more fine-grained differences the job may require. Architect and novelist Donna Goodman works on achieving mutiple uses in her home-office hybrid.

Goodman lives in a converted loft at the edge of Soho in New York City. It used to be a disco, which is why it has a "gigantic bathroom and practically no kitchen. It was very funky." Rather than trying to create a formal entry or have people enter directly into her living space, Goodman chose instead to have people enter directly into her basic workspace. "The back (where the bedroom is) is very private and the front is very public. The work goes between, so there is a clear notion of city and suburb." Keeping her work in the frontstage area and her private life backstage allows Goodman more freedom in her personal area.

Security from theft was a consideration in this home-office design. The neutral work zone visitors see upon entering is simple and sparsely furnished. "I don't want them to know what I have," so all they see when opening the door is what looks like very basic workspace. As you move into the work areas, to the left, you glimpse a magnificent rosewood conference table surrounded by wood, cane, and chrome chairs. To the left two gray art nouveau sofas are side by side against a long wall. Facing them are more chrome and cane conference chairs. None of this can be seen from the entrance.

The feeling is more of being in a workspace than in someone's home; zoning makes it a less personal atmosphere than in most home offices. Goodman wants to convey an impression of professionalism to her clients and visitors; "I used to live in tiny little student-like quarters." Goodman calls her new image "luke-cool"—a personally distinctive but nevertheless slightly formal impression; it shows in her furniture.

The rosewood furniture was designed for a movie producer. "When he moved to Italy he gave it back to me for the price of a few drawings." The richness of the woods, the gray velour art nouveau sofas, and the chrome and cane conference chairs work well to create a "slightly formal" air softened by the loft itself: huge arched windows framed in weathered wood and wonderful aged planking on the floors. The space is neither homey or standard corporate fare. It is minimal without being cold.

Strict zoning of space for specific activities imposes a spatial order that helps Goodman keep track of progress on several projects. She is working on an architectural science-fiction novel, maintains a small architectural practice, and paints. Appropriately then, Goodman maintains a desk for each of these activities in the work

The first thing you see when entering Donna Goodman's loft is what looks like a workspace for four people, but all the desks are Goodman's. There are separate ones for writing, drafting, color work, and business and administrative details.

zone you see immediately upon entering. There is a desk for drafting and architectural work, one where she does the drawings for her book, one at which she writes, and there is even a separate desk for her financial work—keeping tabs on bills and financial records. As Goodman says, "I find that it gets more and more zoned as time goes on. It's to the point where every pile of clothes in every drawer is organized in a particular way. It's that kind of thinking."

This personal work zone contrasts with the social, or client-oriented, area created by the conference table and sofas. "This is where I act like a formal architect: I bring

If you keep moving, you enter a more social world. "Luke-cool" is how Goodman describes it. A formal rosewood conference table, gray art nouveau sofas, and chrome and cane side chairs, combined with stark white walls and the absence of small personal artifacts, create a distinctive, elegant space.

in a client, and we sit around either at the table or on the sofa." It can also function as well as a waiting room or a living room, "depending on how I want to use it." The functional freedom of this social area is in deliberate contrast to the active work area, where all she cared about was "maximum table space."

The space conveys who Goodman is and wants to be in all her working roles. "I wanted a long lean workspace so I could work everywhere. I see the whole thing as flexible. I can add and subtract shelves and all of them have real backs so they can be used to back off a room. They don't have to be pushed up against a wall where the backs cannot be seen." The only function this space does not serve is that of a rough-and-tumble warehouse area where she could "just throw stuff around, weld, wear a mechanic's uniform all the time." For the time being, however, her work roles don't call for such an area.

Since form follows income, the place is not perfect for Goodman, but it is a "good quality place." Goodman wanted a place that was comfortable and that had ample light, space, and views of great distances. The loft satisfies all these criteria. It also creates the impression for clients that "I'm wealthier than I am, and more successful." The loft's formal work area motivates Goodman by reminding her of what she can and wants to do. Controlled comfort and the high level of organization contributes to the sense that "everything has a reason."

The absence of children, a spouse, or friends removes social limitations on the form a workspace can take. Within given economic boundaries you can create a distinctive personal workspace. Goodman has done that, and the two artists that follow have done it as well, in very different ways and with very different economic resources and time perspectives.

PERMEABLE BOUNDARIES

Home has long been a workspace for artists. Where any reasonably comfortable space may suffice for many types of work, painting is more responsive to the quality of space and light surrounding it. A small area hinders work on a large scale, and poor light masks subtle variations in color and shading of an object the artist is rendering. In addition, creative activities like painting, writing, composing, and problem-solving rarely start and stop with the workday clock. Eighteen-hour work days or intense bursts of activity can be followed by apparent total disengagement—but what more often is really a gestation period for new ideas. Creative work is intense, but it is rarely unrelenting.

The benefit of an artist working at home is that his or her workspace is adjacent to living space, making it possible for the artist to get a bite to eat or relax on a sofa without completely losing contact with the work or disrupting a creative thought. Yet the concentration that painting and other creative work requires makes vital some form of spatial separation from other family members and activities.

Artist Natvar Bhavaar's solution to the problem of boundaries in the huge 4,000-square-foot loft he shares with his wife and two infant sons has been to separate his work area from the living area with Japanese-like screens. He made the screens from wood and translucent white fiberglass panels available at any lumberyard or hardware store. By shutting these he can screen his active work area from the living room without cutting off all the light from windows in the living room or totally isolating himself from his family.

If you rent space rather than own it, making permanent additions or customizing furniture to fit a space that you may vacate within a year or two often does not make sense. In temporary situations, use temporary solutions.

Painting at home in one part of a huge rehabilitated loft separated from the main living areas by transparent Japanese-like sliding doors makes it easy for Natvar Bhavsar to work for eighteen or more hours a day, without losing all contact with his family.

When industrial designer and artist Robert O'Neal was in Mexico for only a few months as part of a teaching assignment, he had no desire to become involved in finding and financing a large and expensive space. He did want a place whose light quality and ambience would inspire his painting, while also serving as a temporary home for himself, his wife, and their young son. A tiny studio apartment overlooking a picturesque courtyard turned out to be a delightful solution. O'Neal had merely to spend some time organizing the interior space to comfortably accommodate a working and living arrangement.

The Home Office

This tiny apartment was not ideal, but as a short-term studio it worked well for artist and industrial designer Robert O'Neal. Windows on one side of the apartment provided good natural light, and drawings pinned to another wall generated a space where O'Neal could view works in progress under different lighting conditions and at different angles and distances.

A simple but beautiful paper screen fashioned by O'Neal from a piece of paper folded and cut with designs and then hung between the work-living area and the bedroom create a symbolic boundary between activity zones.

To temporarily screen and define areas O'Neal used a very simple but elegant device. He cut into interesting patterns large sheets of paper, which he hung between the bedroom and the living room-studio to create a delicate screen whose function was largely symbolic. The paper curtain acted as a permeable boundary, distinguishing one area from another. When his family went to bed early, he could remain up working or entertain friends with a sense of separation attained at essentially no cost at all.

SUMMARY

In all these examples one characteristic stands out: effective home offices are highly zoned. Clear distinctions exist between working and living areas, but the boundaries separating them can be more or less permeable, depending on your family situation and the particular work you do. Zoning does several things. First, it separates family members from clients and customers in client-centered home offices. Second, boundaries within the home help establish work territories where interruptions and intrusions are more effectively controlled. It is easier to establish and enforce rules about use when there are physical props that reinforce them. Third, private work territories—even ones where the boundaries are largely symbolic—can motivate and energize you. Fourth, they underscore professional identities and responsibilities. The allocation in your home of scarce resources like space or money for sophisticated equipment can be a sharp reminder to everyone that your work is important.

If your work at home requires meeting with clients, remember that decisions about which furniture, paintings, carpets, and other items you use to decorate your home office will be a compromise. Visitors' impressions must be kept in mind, but you should not sacrifice your own tastes, values, and comfort. You want others to know something about you, but not everything.

If you use your home office for administrative work, storage systems and easy retrieval of information is critical. Since clients or customers impressions are not an issue, do not worry about them. Do what works for you. No matter what work you do at home, this is the one place where you can exercise the greatest amount of control over your workspace. Take advantage of the opportunity. Your office at home should work for you, not you for it.

CONCLUSION

The Successful Office

How you design your office will greatly affect other people's impressions of you—your competence and open-mindedness, your concern for subordinates and your effectiveness among peers. More personally the office has a direct bearing on your comfort, sense of achievement, and satisfaction with your personal identity. By now, we can consider these to be basic management principles, as essential to success as profit sheets and hierarchies. But in designing your workspace to fit a personal workstyle, you will ultimately run up against a collective force—one which organizational theorists call office "culture." Essentially a powerful set of widely held expectations about what is right, appropriate, or acceptable behavior, office culture includes very specific images of the "right" way to work and the particular designs needed to support it.

Office culture varies from one organization to another (even from one department to another within the same company), and it often creates pressure for standard, "one size fits all" office designs. If the culture considers "good" workers to be neat and orderly, personal workspaces will be expected to reflect this image: clean desk and cabinet tops, with everything in its place and a place for everything. A personal style that tends toward the casual (or sloppy) will not fit this culture. On the other hand, if "good" workers are defined by the office culture as "creative" or "independent" or "wild and crazy," then an office with a barber's chair or a desk carved from a redwood burl may be considered highly impressive. The office culture determines the basic characteristics of office design over which you probably have very little control: the size and shape of your office, or whether it's open or closed, private or shared. Yet even within these constraints, and beyond the tools and concepts already noted, you can still make your office work better for you.

If you think for a moment of your workplace as a neighborhood, and this book as a guide to it, then you might say that as you have been reading, you have been walking up and down streets, browsing in stores, admiring the architectural detail of various structures, and imagining how to revitalize your own area. As a result, you now have loads of design ideas, yet you realize that not much can be done about the shape of your roof, for example, or your proximity to neighbors. But what if you could build your dream house—if you could start from scratch?

You would probably look first at the neighborhood, at any nearby parks, roads, schools, stores, libraries, and so on. Why? Because the quality of your life is dependent on them. You spend time in all of these places, and therefore you want them to be accessible, convenient, and pleasant. The same is true of where you work.

In designing your office, therefore, the final step should be to shift focus from your personal territory to a conception of the office as a whole—as a neighborhood of workers. Consider what, in fact, goes on in the office. The work neighborhood is where we meet others and exchange information, ideas, and gossip. Work relationships are built on politics and gamesmanship, friendship and comaradarie. The work community is where we learn what our job is all about and what our friends and co-workers expect of us. It's the place where we sometimes want to be isolated and sometimes want to be in the center of things.

If I were to go ahead and plan the best possible work environment, entirely from the beginning, I'd envision a workspace that trades on the neighborhood concept, that replaces the dream of a single private office, sitting like an isolated farmhouse on a distant plain, with the vision of a city townhouse that is part of an exciting, wider web of people, places and activities. In this environment, neither privacy nor community would be sacrificed for each other.

My notion is built upon the newest advances in office equipment. The office of the future will involve computers and telecommunication technologies that will free people from spatial constraints, and make the notion of work neighborhoods possible. If you are presently working with various kinds of resource materials and files, you are physically bound to the same place as those resources. If all your files are in your office, you need to be there too. (It's one reason moving between your home and the office can be frustrating. At a critical juncture you often don't have the necessary materials.) In modern offices, electronic file systems and portable computers the size of a briefcase can be plugged in anywhere there is electricity and a telephone line. Information is stored in one place but technology allows people access to it as they move from place to place.

Because the computer provides mobility, and because no single workspace can satisfy the myriad functions you and your co-workers do everyday, the concept of a zoned office "neighborhood" makes sense. The goal is to create a network of linked workspaces with each zone designed to serve a distinct function and meet a particular psychological or social need. I would imagine such settings could include a Sanctuary, a Club, a Watering Hole, a Meeting Place, a Library, and a Gym.

Some of the settings, like the Gym, Library, and Watering Hole, are familiar and well-accepted as part of modern office facilities. Places like a comfortable cafeteria or the "Garden Room" that is part of the Arnold and Porter law firm (see Chapter 2) bring together, in a relaxed and informal setting, people who do not get much of a chance to see each other during the day. The more unusual and innovative areas in the plan are the Sanctuary and Club.

· The Sanctuary
In the new office, the opportunity for privacy and personal identity will be widely available. Knowledge workers need the opportunity to shut themselves off from other people and sounds in order to concentrate. Given this, every office worker will have a small, totally

private work room located within a few minutes walking distance from their other "communal" work areas. Large enough for a desk, two chairs, a desktop computer, and minimal storage space, the main purpose of the Sanctuary is to provide a place to get away from it all—at the office. How the Sanctuary is furnished and what goes on within its walls is your concern only; no one besides you, or someone you invite in for a private discussion, should ever have reason to enter. It's the ultimate backstage area in a central office facility. The need for privacy to work effectively is met here, as is the need for identity and stability.

· The Club

Some people may not, however, want a personal Sanctuary. They may prefer working at the Club and using devices like individual stereo systems to screen noise when they need to concentrate. The Club beautifully compliments the privacy of the Sanctuary by providing meaningful social contact and a sense of belonging in a small, tightly-knit work group. Complex problems require complex solutions, and many companies are finding that teams of diverse specialists are better problem-solvers than individuals. People with varying skills and abilities brought together to solve particular problems will require a special place that facilitates the development of strong personal and working relationships. It is in this relatively small work group that the need for meaningful social contact, sharing of ideas and feedback, and a sense of integration into a larger whole can really occur.

Each group, or Club, will therefore be assigned to a work area in which a great deal of time will be spent. The group as a whole can decide how to arrange and decorate their shared work area to reflect their workstyles and values. Thus the Club becomes the focus for group identity among a small number of people. It compliments and extends the personal identity of the Sanctuary. Since it is primarily intended for communication and interaction, comfortable chairs, conference tables, and small desks would be provided as basic appointments. The room itself would be completely private, but within it no areas would be separated by partitions or screens that tend to isolate people.

The Club also provides the person working part-time at home a "home" at work. Portable computer terminals make it easier to work at home without being cut-off from critical sources of data and information. The ability to share written or analytical work with co-workers at the office via video display screens means that you can get feedback on work in progress without having to personally meet with someone. For each part-time worker, clubs create more flexibility and reduce costs for the organization, which should not have to maintain as much individually-assigned space.

Taken together, the beauty of such functionally distinct zones is their variety: they not only accommodate diverse workstyles, they also support individual needs for personal recognition and identity, as well as social needs for a sense of meaningful integration within a social group. Both Club and Sanctuary fulfill social and psychological requirements that tend, now, to be rather inconsistently met.

In fact, the concept of zones very closely resembles how we organize one of society's primary work units: the family. Generally speaking, we live with several different people—mother, father, children, relatives, friends, strangers—all interacting in an ordered fashion to accomplish different tasks: food preparation, storage, maintenance, teaching and learning, supervision, recreation, group meetings, private study. Does all this happen in one big space? Not if it can be avoided.

Different rooms serve different functions: eating in the dining room, food preparation in the kitchen, socializing in the living room, study in bedrooms. Can you imagine trying to assign each family member one space for all the "tasks" they are required to do? The people assigned the living room will find it well-suited to socializing, but horrible for cooking. Children assigned to bedrooms can study effectively, but their isolation from other family members would deprive them of valuable contacts with parents and their friends, and their own siblings, from whom they learn directly and by observation about adult concerns, family values, and acceptable behavior patterns.

Family members move between the different "work areas" in the home as their activities vary. In the process they learn different social roles and develop a sense of themselves as an integrated working unit—exactly what most organizations hope to see happen at work. We learn to leave Dad alone when he's relaxing in the recliner, to send the children to their room when they need to study, and to require everyone to share one family meal together to create a sense of group identity.

THE IMPOSSIBLE DREAM?

If the concept of a zoned office and in particular the idea of a "Club" seem interesting but impractical, consider this example from one of the giants of American industry. In 1974 an experimental production engineering department at IBM developed and implemented the idea of a "non-territorial" or neighborhood style office. It was more extreme than what I am proposing, and it served individual privacy and identity needs less well. Still, was it a failure? To almost everyone's surprise, no!

IBM's non-territorial office put into practice the idea for a series of linked activity zones, which enabled people to move throughout their division over the course of the day as their activities—and work requirements—changed. The premise here was that the opportunity for establishing eye-contact with co-workers is critical to effective discussions.

Not only were all office walls removed at IBM, but so were most desks and other permanent work stations. Only one permanent station remained, occupied by a "central communicator" who handled incoming and outgoing mail, assisted visitors, and operated a switchboard directing calls to the phone nearest the person being called. All work was performed at one of three basic areas within the large room: at laboratory benches and large round tables; in a quiet area enclosed by one wall that had comfortable chairs and could be used for meetings, performance evaluations of work requiring high concentration; and in a totally quiet room which was created from what had formerly been the department head's office! The whole area was attractively and tastefully decorated using carpeting and fabric. Individuals chose to work wherever their needs were best suited.

Despite fears that the loss of the "territorial imperative" would cause widespread dissatisfaction, the change actually increased satisfaction. Employees felt they had more space (even though this had not changed), more privacy, and fewer distractions. The number of different individuals each person talked with more than doubled. Researchers estimated that organizing an office like this would be approximately thirty percent less expensive than one designed in more traditional ways.

I do not advocate the total absence of a personal workspace. Over time, pressure for personal work areas would surely mount. Zoned offices that provide small personal group areas can succeed, however. The benefits of increased group and personal identity, and the opportunity to achieve different levels of privacy and interaction depending on what you are doing at the moment, are very real.

WHO BENEFITS?

Everyone. In such an office it becomes obvious that you are recognized as the most important and expensive resource the organization has. Status is raised for everyone through access to high quality special function rooms such as meeting places, libraries, and gyms. Personal recognition—a key element of status—is provided at a higher level than is now typical through both the Sanctuary and Club work areas. Status and function are integrated, and can both work to promote real effectiveness. Organizations that do everything they can to provide workspace tailored to fit your personal workstyles are maximizing the investment they have made in you. It will work both for you and the organization.

What we can do now is plan for the future by setting up the space and the "tools" for such areas, if even informally. Moreover, we can start designing our dream office by talking about its benefits with colleagues and others in the office. Out of such measures, the office of the future comes closer to being a reality. Designed for such diversity, the modern office becomes a genuine tool of the trade.

INDEX

Index

Index